Psalms for Recovery

Psalms for Recovery

Meditations for Strength and Hope

Barbara Stephens
"Mama Hug"

Abundant Life Ministries
Pensacola, Florida

Second Edition
Published by Abundant Life Ministries
ISBN 978-0-578-04509-2

For more information, contact:
Abundant Life Ministries
P.O. Box 4474
Pensacola, FL 32507
(850) 497-8505
www.mamahug.org

Introduction

Recovery is a simple, uncomplicated word. There's nothing frightening about just saying it or seeing it, but to experience recovery may evoke every emotion known to humankind, especially at the beginning of the journey.

It doesn't matter what your drug of choice has been—alcohol, drugs, food, sex, gambling, smoking, or relationships, you may have a certain amount of fear and anxiety because you are changing your entire life-style.

Recovery begins when the pain of remaining addicted/codependent has become greater than the fear and pain of change. A child may experience a toothache but refuses to tell anyone because of his or her fear for the dentist. Until the pain of that toothache becomes greater than the fear, the child will continue to suffer. As the pain continues to intensify, the dentist begins to sound better and better. When our addiction/codependency begins to cause more pain than it relieves, recovery begins to look like a possible solution.

*The Twelve Steps**

1. We admitted we were powerless over [addiction], that our lives had become unmanageable.

2. Came to believe that a Power greater than ourselves could restore us to sanity.

3. Made a decision to turn our will and our lives over to the care of God *as we understood Him.*

4. Made a searching and fearless moral inventory of ourselves.

5. Admitted to God, to ourselves, and to another human being the exact nature of our wrongs.

6. Were entirely ready to have God remove all these defects of character.

7. Humbly asked Him to remove our shortcomings.

8. Made a list of all persons we had harmed, and became willing to make amends to them all.

9. Made direct amends to such people whenever possible, except when to do so would injure them or others.

10. Continued to take personal inventory and when we were wrong promptly admitted it.

11. Sought through prayer and meditation to improve our conscious contact with God *as we understood Him,* praying only for the knowledge of His will for us and the power to carry that out.

12. Having had a spiritual awakening as the result of these steps, we tried to carry these messages [to others], and to practice these principles in all our affairs.

This book is a daily source of strength for the recovering person. It uses the Twelve Steps and combines them with the Book of Psalms to bring hope, strength, and correction.

This book began as my own personal journal of recovery in October 1988. I had been without my "drug of choice" (relationships) for eleven days, and I was in the most emotional turmoil I had ever known. Turning to the Psalms and seeing the Twelve Steps so plainly in many of them encouraged me. I share with you what was a gift to me on one of the most difficult and yet rewarding journeys I've experienced.

Barbara Sue Ward Stephens
"Mama Hug"

Psalm 1

*Blessed is the man who does not walk
in the counsel of the wicked. (v. 1)*

Our addictive/codependent thinking is wicked because it is not in our best interest. Sometimes friends and relatives who are not recovering or do not understand the Twelve-Step program may give counsel that is unhelpful or unwise. Therefore, we need to look to God for our direction, for our counsel. As we draw strength from Him and from His Word, we will become stronger and experience victory. Our support groups are another source of understanding, love, and helpful counsel; and we are able to stand strong as we listen with an open heart to others' stories of recovery.

Still another source of wise direction is our sponsor. All of these people make up a network of comfort, encouragement, and inspiration so that we do not have to turn to the counsel of those who do not understand.

*Lord, help me to use wisely
the tools of recovery.*

Psalm 2

Blessed are all who take refuge in him. (v. 12)

Probably at no other time in our lives will we be quite as vulnerable as we are during the first stage of our recovery. Probably at no other time in our lives will our pain be any greater. What a comfort to realize that at these times we can take refuge in Him. When our emotions are in a million pieces, we can take refuge in His Word. When there is no other, He is there—day after day, after day. When we are most vulnerable, we can run to the safety of our Father. When we are hurting, we can run into the strong tower of His acceptance. He is our refuge, and with Him we can make it.

Father, teach me that at my most vulnerable
times, I can run to You.

Psalm 3

O Lord, how many are my foes!
How many rise up against me!
Many are saying of me, "God will not deliver him."
But you are a shield around me,
O Lord; you bestow glory
on me and lift up my head. To the Lord
I cry aloud, and he answers from his holy hill. . . .
from the Lord comes deliverance. May your
blessing be on your people. (vv. 1-4; 8)

Many days we have felt overwhelmed in our recovery. Our addiction/codependency is too big to be conquered. But God isn't hampered by what we feel; His promise doesn't hinge on what we feel. When He says He'll do something, He does it.

We find Step Two in verse 8 of this Psalm: We came to believe that God could restore us to sane living. God and our cooperation with His plan to deliver us are sure to produce health and victory.

Lord, help me to realize that feelings are temporary.

Psalm 4

Answer me when I call to you, O my righteous God.
Give me relief from my distress; be
merciful to me and hear my prayer.
How long, O men, will you turn my glory into
shame? How long will you
love delusions and seek false gods?
Know that the Lord has set apart the godly for
himself; the Lord will hear when I call to him.
In your anger do not sin; when you are on your beds,
search your hearts and be silent.
Offer right sacrifices, and trust in the Lord.
Many are asking, "Who can show us any good?"
Let the light of your face shine upon us, O Lord.
You have filled my heart with greater joy
than when their grain and new wine abound.
I will lie down and sleep in peace, for you
alone, O Lord, make me dwell in safety. (vv. 1-8)

Whether emotionally dependent or addicted, we are in such distress that we call out to God. At one time, the drug or person may have eased our pain; but now there is no relief. Still in denial, we continue to hold the illusion that maybe once more the pain can be eased by returning to the addiction. Hitting bottom brings us to the truth that we must turn our lives and wills over to God. The outcome is that God can and will fill the depths within with joy and contentment. No drug or relationship could ever do that for us on a permanent basis.

Father, in my distress, give me courage to follow Your direction.

Psalm 5

The Prayer of the Recovering Person

Give ear to my words, O Lord, consider my sighing. Listen to my cry for help, my King and my God, for to you I pray. In the morning, O Lord, you hear my voice; in the morning I lay my requests before you and wait in expectation. You are not a God who takes pleasure in evil; with you the wicked cannot dwell. The arrogant cannot stand in your presence; you hate all who do wrong. But I, by your great mercy, will come into your house; in reverence will I bow down. Lead me, O Lord, in your righteousness because of my enemies—make straight your way before me. Not a word from their mouth can be trusted. . . . For surely, O Lord, You bless the righteous; you surround them with your favor as with a shield. (vv. 1-5; 7-9; 12)

This Psalm may sound vaguely familiar to the recovering person, comparable to prayers cried out to God in the midst of discouragement. Many times we lay out an agenda for God to meet; and when it does not happen as we planned, we lose heart. But the secret of peace is to wait for God to give us our agenda and then to have a heart full of expectancy. Prayer is another way of taking refuge on those tough days, and taking refuge produces gladness and a song in our hearts. We love His name, rejoice, and are blessed because we are protected by His favor.

In Step Two on our journey of recovery, He places a shield about us that will assure our victory.

Father, remind me that soon I will be glad
and I will sing again.

Psalm 6

O Lord, do not rebuke me in your anger
or discipline me in your wrath. Be merciful to me,
Lord, for I am faint; O Lord, heal me,
for my bones are in agony. My soul is in anguish.
How long, O Lord, how long?
Turn, O Lord, and deliver me;
save me because of your unfailing love. (vv. 1-4)

Recovering from our addiction/codependency brings us in touch with feelings that overwhelm us. It is difficult for us to understand that God isn't out to "get us."

- We fear God's anger.
- We need His mercy.
- We are weak.
- We need His healing.
- We feel He has left us.
- We need deliverance.

After being "sober" several days, we can begin to *feel* again. Our feelings say we're being punished. We are faint; we are weary. We need the God of the Second Step to restore us.

Our hearts and souls are in such pain. How long will we suffer? (Remember the child with the toothache.)

Our symptoms are so painful that we weep; we cry. After we cry so much, our eyes are blurred. We are in sorrow because of our addiction. We are entirely ready to have God remove all these defects, as in Step Six. God's unfailing love will deliver us. We will be free.

Father, remind me often that I will enjoy a life of freedom once more.

Psalm 7

O Lord my God, I take refuge in you;
save and deliver me from all who pursue me
[my addiction/codependence], or they will tear me
like a lion and rip me to pieces
with no one to rescue me. (vv. 1-2)

Until there is a rescuer, we keep on in our addictive/codependent life-styles. We must experience the consequences fully before we will truly recover. Until then, we continue self-defeating thinking and behaving. When we have "bottomed out," we will turn our lives and wills over to God as we understand Him.

Addiction/codependency is like a lion: It shows absolutely no mercy as it rips and tears our lives apart. Dare we not continue on this journey into recovery?

Lord, give me strength to continue the journey, even
on difficult days.

Psalm 8

When I consider your heavens, the work of your
fingers, the moon and the stars, which you have
set in place, what is a man that you are mindful of
him, the son of man that you care for him?
You made him a little lower than the heavenly beings
and crowned him with glory and honor. You made
him ruler over the works of your hands; you put
everything under his feet. (vv. 3-6)

We can trust our lives to the care of God. We can
depend on Him for whatever we need. When we
consider all that He has made and done, it is baffling
to realize that we are important to Him.

God, our Father, has ordained great things for each of
His children, but until we are able to reach out of our
addiction/codependency, we will never experience
those things. It's amazing that He gives us dominion,
ability to rule over the works of his hands; but we are
powerless over our addiction. That powerlessness
puts us in a position for a great and mighty God to
take charge of our lives and bring us along in our
journeys of recovery.

Father, than You for loving me into recovery with
"tough love."

Psalm 9

*My enemies turn back, they stumble and perish
before you. . . . The Lord is a refuge for the
oppressed, a stronghold in times of trouble.
Those who know your name will trust in you,
for you, Lord, have never forsaken
those who seek you. . . . For he who avenges
blood remembers; he does not ignore
the cry of the afflicted. (vv. 3; 9-10; 12)*

Because God is working with us in our recovery, we
want to praise Him and tell others, as in Step Twelve.
Our addictions gradually lose their tight hold on our
lives. Many different emotions and pains may have
encouraged our addictions. As God heals and we
work with Him, even the memory of them is healed.
We can turn them over to Him. We can hide in Him.
God will not abandon us. God will not ignore us
when we turn to Him, even when our addictions
scream. In our great need, we can turn to Him; even
in our affliction, we can hope. He is able.

*Father, You are able, especially when I am
powerless.*

Psalm 10

*Why, O Lord, do you stand far off? Why do you hide
yourself in times of trouble? . . .
His victims are crushed, they collapse; they fall
under his strength. (vv. 1; 10)*

On those days when our addiction is screaming, we
may feel that God stands far away, that He hides
from us when we are in trouble.

Many times the enemy (the addicted self) craves, in
our hearts and souls, for the relief we once knew.
When we're really into addiction, we don't seek God:
Our minds are so caught up in "stuff" that there is no
room for thoughts of God.

But somewhere deep inside us, a part has begun to
recover; and God keeps reminding us that He isn't
absent, even when we can't feel Him.

*Father, give me strength to endure this temporary
craving.*

Psalm 11

The Lord is in his holy temple; the Lord is on his heavenly throne. He observes the sons of men; his eyes examine them. The Lord examines the righteous, but the wicked and those who love violence his soul hates. . . . For the Lord is righteous, he loves justice; upright men will see his face. (vv. 4-5; 7)

At Step Six, we were entirely ready to have God remove all these defects. Our only hope now is to learn how to do this.

In the midst of our pain, we take refuge in the Lord. Our wounded souls constantly pull and beg and long. "Stinking thinking" shoots from the darkness within us, trying to gain control.

God doesn't abandon us in our struggle. He sees us, knows us, and is moved by compassion for what we feel.

Because of what our addiction/codependence does to us, He hates it. He will purge from our beings the very wound or root that has caused us to seek the drug of choice, be it people, drugs, alcohol, sex, gambling, success, food, or nicotine.

The Lord is righteous; He loves justice and truth. As we are able to see that He is not mad at us but at the addiction that has nearly destroyed our lives, we are able to admit our problem with honesty, openness, and willingness.

Addiction stole our joy, our happiness, our lives, and even our wills—but God restores back to us all that was lost.

Lord, teach me to be honest with myself, open to You, and willing to risk with others.

Psalm 12

O Lord, you will keep us safe and protect us from such people forever. (v. 7)

God cares that we are struggling with recovery. He cares that at times the addictive personality almost gains control, and He protects us from those who would pull us back.

God will keep us safe; He will protect us from the pull of our addiction/codependency. Our willingness to follow when and where He leads, to wait when He isn't moving, and to obey when He speaks assures us of another day of recovery.

Lord, teach me when to wait and when to follow.

Psalm 13

How long, O Lord? Will you forget me forever? How long will you hide your face from me? How long must I wrestle with my thoughts and everyday have sorrow in my heart? How long will my enemy triumph over me? Look on me and answer, O Lord my God. Give light to my eyes, or I will sleep in death; my enemy will say, "I have overcome him," and my foes will rejoice when I fall. But I trust in your unfailing love; my heart rejoices in your salvation. I will sing to the Lord, for he has been good to me. (vv. 1-6)

Emotionally this is the way it feels:

- God has forgotten us (v. 1).
- God is hiding His face.
- We wrestle with our thoughts (v. 2).
- Every day we have sorrow in our hearts.
- How long will our enemy triumph over us?
- We need to hear from God (v. 3).
- We need insight before we crack emotion-ally.
- The enemy is laughing (v. 4).
- We *must* trust His unfailing love (v. 5).
- We will sing again because He has been good to us (v. 6).

Lord, teach me the secret of one day at a time.

Psalm 14

The fool says in his heart, "There is no God."
They are corrupt, their deeds are vile;
there is no one who does good.
The Lord looks down from heaven on the sons of men
to see if there are any who understand,
any who seek God. All have turned aside,
they have together become corrupt;
there is no one who does good, not even one.
Will evildoers never learn—those who devour my
people as men eat bread and who do not call on the
Lord? There they are, overwhelmed with dread, for
God is present in the company of the righteous.
You evildoers frustrate the plans of the poor,
but the Lord is their refuge. (vv.1-6)

Step Two tells us we came to believe that a Power greater than ourselves could restore us to sanity. Maybe another word for insanity would be *fool*. When we live with the belief that we can do our own thing—or run our lives—our whole lives are a mess. Our deeds are vile, and we find it impossible to do good.

For many addicts, this is a very hard lesson to learn. But until we come to the awareness that God is and that He can restore us to sanity, we will flounder and fall. Stability is the result of acknowledging God as the source of our recovery.

O God, remind me that I'm not big enough without You.

Psalm 15

Lord, who may dwell in your sanctuary?
Who may live on your holy hill? He whose walks is
blameless and who does what is righteous,
who speaks the truth from his heart and
has no slander on his tongue,
who does his neighbor no wrong and casts no slur on
his fellow man, who despises a vile man but
honors those who fear the Lord, Who keeps his oath
even when it hurts, who lends his money without
usury and does not accept a bribe against the
innocent. He who does these things will never be
shaken. (vv. 1-5)

It is one thing to know *about* God; it is quite another to *know* Him. Prayer and meditation upon His Word help us get to know Him.

And yet, Lord, even when we do our best to get to know You, sometimes our own fears and wrong beliefs interfere. We want to come close to Your sanctuary. We desire to live on Your holy hill. But our own thoughts tell us that, because of the mess we've made of our lives, You would not want us anywhere near you. Lord, in our sane moments we know that isn't true. Teach us how to know You and how to really trust You.

In recovery, we are learning how to live with other less-than-perfect people, and we are learning how to speak our feelings without crushing someone else. Becoming trustworthy is often a difficult task because of our past record, and yet that is such an important part of recovery. So we will endure the doubts that others have about us; one day we will be beyond this. Today we are willing.

Father, draw my recovering heart closer to You through meditation and prayer.

Psalm 16

Keep me safe, O God, for in you I take refuge.
I said to the Lord, "You are my Lord;
apart from you I have no good thing." (vv. 1-2)

Those who were so addicted/codependent may find it strange to realize that apart from the Lord we have nothing good. Left to our own devices, we will destroy everything good that comes our way. But we are very aware that success in recovery requires a partnership. God plus the one recovering person, daily walking out the stages of recovery, will surely bring victory. We can't do it without God, and He doesn't need recovery. So it's a twosome.

As long as we keep the Lord active in our recovery and hold on to Him, we will not be shaken; but when we think we can do it alone, watch out!

Some days our hearts are so glad that recovery is now our life-style, and we rejoice. Our bodies begin to relax and rest securely because we are confident that God will not abandon us to the grave.

As recovery progresses, our lives are filled with joy because we begin to *really enjoy* being in His presence. Today we take refuge in the Lord.

Lord, give me constant awareness that recovery is partnership.

Psalm 17

Though you probe my heart and examine me at night,
thought you test me, you will find nothing. I have
resolved that my mouth will not sin. (v. 3)

Step Ten reminds us to continue to take a personal inventory and, when we are wrong, to promptly admit it. We must allow God to probe the depths of our hearts and examine us. So often we are able to rationalize our behavior and thinking, and we excuse ourselves. So in recovery, we must be willing to expose ourselves to God, even when we think we're coming along okay. Growth only comes as we open ourselves up to Him, knowing that He will not reject even the worst about us. When we realize that all of our personal self-help, and self-improvement efforts have not truly changed us, then we are more willing to allow Him to test us.

Our mortal enemy is our disease of addiction/codependency. Addiction/codependency has its own agenda. Addiction/codependency is concerned about only one thing—to take over, control, defeat, and destroy. But what a comfort to know that God looks at us, even in recovery, even on not-so-good days, as the apple of His eye and that He hides us in the shadow of His wings when the addiction/codependency is pulling at our very hearts. God *will* restore us to sanity.

Father, admitting I am wrong is so hard—give me strength to do it.

Psalm 18

*I love you, O Lord, my strength. The Lord is my rock,
my fortress and my deliverer; my
God is my rock, in whom I take refuge. He is my
shield and the horn of my salvation, my stronghold. I
call to the Lord, who is worthy of praise, and I am
saved from my enemies. (vv. 1-3)*

Some days of recovery are just bad days. Pain overwhelms us, and our hurt and grief scream. On those days, it would be so easy to slip, to go back to the old ways.

But on those days when we are too weak, He is our strength. When we are shaky, He is our rock. When we need security, He is our fortress. When we need a safe place, He is our refuge. And wonder of wonders, He is committed to our recovery. Even on those days when we know for sure we'll never make it, He stands firm.

Just think: God, our Father, the Creator of this universe, is interested in our recovery. Only He can keep our lamp burning, and He does turn our darkness into light.

God, on bad days, hold on tightly to me.

Psalm 19

*The heavens declare the glory of God; the skies
proclaim the work of His hands. Day after day they
pour forth speech; night after night they display
knowledge. . . .*
*May the words of my mouth and the meditation of my
heart be pleasing in your sight. . . . (vv. 1-2; 14)*

In recovery, it is easy to get so caught up in
programs, sponsors, and meetings that we forget to
improve our conscious contact with God. This is a
serious downfall that can lead to relapse if we are not
cautious. This Psalm tells us a good way to improve
conscious contact: through nature. Take time to enjoy
God's love-gift of Creation. Walk in the woods;
listen to the water rushing in a stream; look at the
stars and moon; smell the flowers. Slow down and
take time to hear what nature tells us about God.
Drive through the country, or in the mountains or
take some other scenic route and enjoy the voice of
nature. Watch for sunsets and sunrises and beautiful
cloud formations, and on rainy days, look for those
beautiful rainbows. Watch the birds and animals, and
enjoy the beautiful world our Father created for us.

*On busy days, Lord, speak to me in ways
that I will hear.*

Psalm 20

May the Lord answer you when you are in distress;
may the name of the God of Jacob protect you.
May he send you help from the sanctuary and grant
you support from Zion.
May he remember all your sacrifices and accept
your burnt offerings.
May he give you the desire of your heart and make
all your plans succeed.
We will shout for joy when you are victorious and
will lift up your banners in the name of our God.
May the Lord grant all your requests. (vv. 1-5)

Just as Step One is important, so is Step Twelve. In the continuing of the recovery process, we reach out to others; and this Psalm is a prayer for others in recovery. Our aim should be to constantly hold up in prayer those who are struggling with recovery. May our prayer be that God will answer those in distress. May He protect those who are struggling. May He send help and grant support. May He remember the sacrifices, give the desires of the heart, and make His plans succeed. May He grant the requests according to His will.

Together we will shout for joy when we are victorious, and we will proclaim to other addicts/codependents that recovery is a real possibility for those who turn to Him.

God, use me to reach out to others who are struggling with recovery.

Psalm 21

*O Lord, the king rejoices in your strength. How great
is his joy in the victories you give! (v. 1)*

Think of the "king" in this Psalm as ourselves. When
we finally do learn how to "turn it over," we can
learn to rejoice in His strength. He gives victory, and
we begin to have joy as we take each step out of
addiction, out of the sickness and out of the pain.
When the desire of our heart is recovery, or
wholeness, He begins to work to that end. No matter
what a mess our lives may have been in, God
welcomes us to come as we are. He pours out rich
blessings even though we are so sick and messed up
at the time; He pours blessings on us even when we
do not realize it. God gives us life when we have
been consumed with death. God grants us victories
each day, one step at a time. Each sober minute is a
victory.

When we trust in the Lord and realize His unfailing
love, we will not be shaken for long. God will give us
strength, courage, and power to live sober lives. Our
addictive nature sets us up to fall, but God helps us to
be winners.

*O Lord, grant that I may follow Your pathway
to victory.*

Psalm 22

*My God, my God, why have you forsaken me? Why
are you so far from saving me, so far from the words
of my groaning? O my God, I cry out by day, but you
do not answer, by night, and am not silent. (vv. 1-2)*

Although this is a prophecy about Jesus and His
Crucifixion, it is also the cry of the suffering one's
heart.

The desperate cry of "My God, why have You
forsaken me?" is the actual feeling we have from
time to time. In our pain, it seems that surely God has
abandoned us.

Many times it seems that God is not listening and that
He is not doing anything to help us. We have seen
with our eyes the deliverance of others from a life-
style of addiction; we have heard their stories. God
delivered them; they are walking in recovery. So
what is wrong with us? Our own thoughts mock us,
telling us that that we are foolish to trust in the Lord
to rescue and deliver us.

Yet God delivered us from our mother's womb; He
taught us that we can trust; He has been faithful from
our conception. He will not let us be defeated now.
Our emotions tell us He is absent; trouble seems

much closer that He does, and yet no one else can really help.

Addiction seems to have the power of a bull, especially at the beginning of our recovery. The pull of our emotions and the physical pain seem like lions tearing their prey. Even our bones cry out in pain. Realizing that only God can help us at this point, we can reach out to Him, even when our emotions tell us that He is far away.

We want recovery to produce instant happiness, but recovery is "here a little, there a little," . . . day by day.

Lord, remind me that all of life is
"here a little, there a little."

Psalm 23

The Lord is my shepherd, I shall not be in want. (v. 1)

Actually, only God can fill the longing that previously we tried to drown in our addiction/co-dependency. Yet, we often think we need *someone who is touchable,* someone who can "fix" our pain. When we are caught up in the fantasy, we begin to seek the "someone." Until we come to grips with the knowledge that no person can reach the depths of us or stop the pain and longing, we will not recover. The fantasy must die so that we can once and for all reach out to the *only* One who can face the longing with us.

Even though the pain is at times more than we think we can bear—even when the pain screams that God is absent, He is still present. He is with us, even when we are sure He is not. After all, He promised.

As we learn to face the loneliness and longing with Him, needs that have driven us are eased and finally met; and we are free to take further steps in recovery. Day by day and minute by minute, we come to realize that He is able and willing to meet the needs of our hearts so that we actually lack nothing.

*Father, fill my empty longing with Yourself
and Your love.*

Psalm 24

Who may ascend the hill of the Lord?
Who may stand in his holy place?
He who has clean hands and a pure heart,
who does not lift up his soul to an idol
or swear by what is false. (vv. 3-4)

Coming to know God is a very important step in recovery. Much of what we know from our past is clouded by misinformation and must be replaced by accurate facts. God is so powerful. He created the world; surely He can handle our lives, our recoveries. He can be trusted to take us from the lowest pit of addiction to the heights of recovery—but only as we allow Him to lead us, only as we are willing to follow.

Progressive recovery frees us from the idol of addiction/codependency. But we have to remind ourselves that recovery is progressive, and we cannot progress unless we are willing to take those daily steps.

Father, help me take steps when sitting
would be easier.

Psalm 25

To you, O Lord, I lift up my soul; in you I trust,
O my God. Do not let me be put to shame,
nor let my enemies triumph over me. No one whose
hope is in you will ever be put to shame. . . .
Remember not the sins of my youth and my rebellious
ways; according to your love remember me, for you
are good, O Lord. (vv. 1-3; 7)

This is the prayer of the recovering: "I lift up my soul," (but only after our souls become so troubled and diseased).

When we were in so much emotional pain, we had to trust someone; so we chose to trust You, Lord. Do not let us be defeated by our addiction/codependency. Lord, we don't really know You, and we're not sure of how to walk in Your ways, yet You are our only hope. When we look at our lives, we only deserve Your anger and punishment. We have sinned, and we have been in rebellion and have sought out wrong ways to stop our pain.

We need Your forgiveness even though we do not deserve it. Only You, God, can release our feet from the snare of addiction.

One of the greatest fears of codependent/emotionally dependent relationships is that of being alone—the fear of abandonment.

O Lord, free us from the anguish we feel, the deep emotional upheaval we experience; You are our hope. Together we can!

Father, it is a joy to know that we are a team working together on my recovery.

Psalm 26

*My feet stand on level ground; in the great assembly
I will praise the Lord. (v. 12)*

My feet stand on level ground. Making a fearless,
searching, moral inventory of ourselves, as in Step
Four, will certainly bring us to an awareness of our
humanity. Any pride or ego trip we may have been
on while living in addiction/codependency comes to a
screeching halt. As we look at where we have been,
there is absolutely no room to look down at others or
to judge anyone else. At the foot of the Cross, we all
stand on level ground. As painful as the searching,
fearless moral inventory is, it is not as painful as
remaining the same. Once more we are called upon to
face ourselves, to face what we have done. Then we
can admit these faults and allow God to remove
them.

Our addictive/codependent nature (behavior) wants to
blame someone else for all of the ills of this life, but
healing will not begin until we are willing to take
responsibility for our behavior and make amends
where we can. Then God can remove these character
defects from us. Pulling these "weeds" from our lives
leaves room for the good fruit to grow.

*God, may I not be content to stay the same but
constantly grow.*

Psalm 27

The Lord is my light and my salvation—
whom shall I fear? The Lord is the stronghold of my
life—of whom shall I be afraid?
When evil men advance against me to devour my
flesh, when my enemies and my foes attack me,
they will stumble and fall. . . . Do not hide your face
from me, do not turn your servant away in anger;
you have been my helper.
Do not reject me or forsake me, O God, my Savior.
Though my father and mother forsake me, the Lord
will receive me. (vv. 1-2; 9 10)

The Lord is our stronghold, and unlike the stronghold of addiction, the Lord dispels our unreasonable fears. For many years we have feared everything and everyone, but whom do we fear now? Ourselves.

From time to time, even in recovery, our addictive natures beg and coax and at last attack. But we still do not have to fear. Even when our addiction wants us to turn back, we can still be confident that God is not afraid of the day of trouble. He will keep us safe in His dwelling, in the shelter of His tabernacle. We will triumph over our enemy, this addictive personality.

In our distress, we forget that He is near. On some days, it seems that we can't find Him. Addictive relationships are based on the fear of abandonment and rejection. We cannot have those needs met totally today, but God can ease the fear.

Recovery is important enough to wait for and walk through.

Lord, be a light when my dark emotions
cloud my way.

Psalm 28

Hear my cry for mercy as I call to you
for help, as I lift up my hands
toward your Most Holy Place. (v. 2)

Our emotions speak. Many times in our pain and
frustration, we call out to the Lord and really expect
Him not to hear us. We feel unworthy because of our
past failures, broken promises, and defeated lives.
We are disgusted with ourselves, and we feel sure
that He must be, too.

We can each easily say, "I am turning my life, as is,
over to God." But this is quite another thing to
accomplish. It means coming to someone who knows
us completely and trusting that He does want us. It
means risking the ultimate rejection; what a task,
what a muscle-builder for faith! We are reminded
that thousands before us have felt the same way; and
when they risked all, they found the Man of Sorrows
waiting with arms opened wide. He will not turn us
away, and we do not even have to beg Him to accept
us.

Father, help me to run into Your accepting arms.

Psalm 29

*The Lord gives strength to his people; the Lord
blesses his people with peace. (v. 11)*

Only God can change our turmoil into peace, and
only He can bring strength into our weakness. But
even God cannot do these things for us unless we
have put aside our denial and have embraced the
reality of our inability to fix our lives or the lives of
those with whom we have been codependent.

Peace comes when we submit our lives and wills to
the care of God. Peace is the result of surrender just
as turmoil is the result of struggle. Struggle is the
result of exerting our wills.

We can *seem* strong; we can *look* strong; but only
God can strengthen our weakness. So we bring all
that we are and all that we are not to Him and allow
Him to add to us what we lack and remove what we
do not need. Yes, God may remove something we are
sure we need to live happy and fulfilled lives. But we
trust Him, by an act of our wills, to do exactly what is
good and necessary to promote wholeness.

*O God, help me face the truth that I
can't do this alone.*

Psalm 30

When I felt secure, I said, "I will never be shaken."
(v. 6)

Only when our lives are safely in the hands of God can we ever experience true security. In that embrace, we will never be shaken. Notice, it doesn't say we will never *feel shaky*, or *feel shaken*. What we feel in our emotions is not fact but is merely a report of what is happening inside us. Emotions can be the result of something as simple as not eating correctly or on time. Emotions can change with the words or body language of someone we need to affirm us. But because emotions are fickle and subject to change without prior notice, we must remind ourselves that we are held in God's strong embrace, even when our souls tumble uncontrollably.

When we feel that God is not near, we are dismayed. But our feelings can be corrected by what we are saying to ourselves. So we can meditate on the promises of God rather than on "what if's" or "should have's."

Lord, remind me today that emotions change quickly,
but You are steadfast.

Psalm 31

In you, O Lord, I have taken refuge; let me never be put to shame; deliver me in your righteousness. (v. 1)

Shame is one of the most malignant and controlling emotions we can experience. Shame brings us to the misconception that what and who we are is wrong. In recovery, shame is deadly. Shame is a stealer of our personhood.

Many times this deep sense of shame is what first made us reach out to our drug of choice to ease the inner feeling. When what we are is bad, there is little hope. If only what we *do* is bad or wrong, we can hope to change our behavior. But shame says that *we* are wrong or bad.

Only God can restore our sense of dignity, and this begins when we can see that He truly wants to help us. The more aware we become of His desire to be close to us, the less shame we feel. Shame is healed as we continue to come to Him, as we are, and find Him to be completely accepting and totally non-condemning.

O God, remove my feelings of shame and help me to forgive myself.

Psalm 32

I will instruct you and teach you in the way you should go; I will counsel you and watch over you. Do not be like the horse or mule, which have no understanding but must be controlled by bit and bridle or they will not come to you. Many are the woes of the wicked, but the Lord's unfailing love surrounds the man who trusts in him. (vv. 8-10)

God speaks to our hearts just exactly what we need to hear. On some days in recovery, we seem to have lost our direction. Our emotions get topsy-turvy, and we become disoriented. Yet on these days God says, "I will instruct you and teach you in the way you should go." Our Father will take us through step by step until once more our lives are stable and we feel confident. When we don't know which way to go—when the night is so dark we can't see—He will not desert us. God knows the way through the sometimes winding maze of recovery.

On days when things are better, we have a tendency to run ahead of God; and in His great love, He holds on to us, even when it seems He is cramping our style. Just as parents are sometimes forced to restrain their children, many times it is in our best interest for God to restrain us.

But always the Lord's unfailing and unconditional love surrounds us, be it in our time of personal inventory, confession, or lack of direction. He surrounds us with His care.

Father, help me to refocus my recovery today.

Psalm 33

For the word of the Lord is right and true; He is faithful in all he does. The Lord loves righteousness and justice; the earth is full of his unfailing love. . . . For he spoke, and it came to be; he commanded, and it stood firm. (vv. 4-5; 9)

In the early stages of recovery, we may feel overwhelmed by the pain of our newly awakened feelings. Our drug of choice has kept us conveniently numbed. It has been so long since we have experienced emotions at all. On days when our pain seems too big, we may have to consciously turn our thoughts to His promises. Meditating on those promises does not instantly bring our lives into perfection, but stinking thinking must stop somewhere. To redirect our thoughts, to focus our thoughts on something stable, does eventually bring order to our disordered lives. At first, we can only concentrate for short periods of time; but if we are faithful to this discipline, eventually we will find that our thinking is easier to turn in the right direction. Our thoughts do create many of our emotions.

Lord, today help me to remember Your promise of victory.

Psalm 34

The Lord is close to the brokenhearted and saves
those who are crushed in spirit. . . . The Lord
redeems his servants; no one will be condemned who
takes refuge in him.(vv. 18; 22)

Not one hurting heart goes unnoticed by Him. He is
touched by the feelings of our infirmities, and what
could be more descriptive of infirmity than the addic-
tive/codependent person? How His heart reaches out
to His struggling children over and over! Even in the
midst of our addiction/codependency, He longs for us
to be whole.

Many times we feel that He hates those of us who are
addicts/codependents; but He doesn't. He hates that
which is stealing the gift of life from us.

He rescues those who have been crushed in spirit. Is
anyone more crushed in spirit than those who have
been involved in addiction/codependency? Our own
wrong choices have often served as the crushing
blow. Yet our Father reaches out to save us even
then, even from ourselves.

No one, absolutely no one, will be condemned who
takes refuge in Him. No matter where we have been,
no matter what we have done, no matter how far we

have fallen—what a promise! His love reaches out to us, even into the pit of despair to which our addiction/codependency has taken us. His love reaches past all of the protective walls we have built and reminds us, "I will not condemn you." Our Father will not condemn us, but what about our own attitude and condemnation? It is so easy for us to hate and to punish ourselves, but that attitude is often projected onto our Father. We condemn ourselves; others may condemn us; but in His hands there is not one tiny bit of condemnation. This freedom from condemnation gives us strength to make amends; the security of acceptance makes it possible to face ourselves and our harmful behavior.

Lord, help me accept myself as human and forgive myself for my humanness.

Psalm 35

Contend, O Lord, with those who contend with me;
fight against those who fight against me. (v. 1)

One of the big things in addiction/codependency is the tendency to blame our pain on someone else, anyone else. It is most uncomfortable to take responsibility for our own mess. Therefore, we want to fight with those around us; we are angry and often want revenge on those we feel have caused our plight. What we are dealing with in recovery is not a person, place, or thing. We are dealing with addiction/codependency.

Addiction/codependency is our mortal enemy. Addiction/codependency is the disease; it is the destroyer. To fight others is unprofitable. We must face ourselves and our disease; we must begin to take responsibility for where we are. Then we must give control to God, who can save us from ourselves *and* our disease.

Lord, it is easier to blame others, but I won't recover
unless I take responsibility for my behavior.
Please help me.

Psalm 36

How priceless is your unfailing love! Both high and
low among men find refuge in the
shadow of your wings. (v. 7)

There is no partiality with God: Whoever comes, He takes in; whoever is needy, He accepts. We who knew only death and emptiness find life, and He gives us light to see.

God holds on to us even when the cravings of our heart want to yield to the addiction/codependency. God accepts the high and mighty, and God accepts the person of low estate. Whoever we are, He does give us refuge.

Lord, help me to put as high a value
on my life as You do.

Psalm 37

If the Lord delights in a man's way,
he makes his steps firm. (v. 23)

Giving God control is a difficult and fearful thing for
those who have spent so much time and effort trying
to be in control. But this is the big step that begins the
process of recovery and the daily step that keeps us
on the journey.

Yes, we may indeed stumble and fall; we may make
mistakes; we may lose our way. But the good news is
that, even if we do, God still holds on to us. He can
set us back on the right path; He can balance us; He
can stabilize us. God will make these tottering,
stumbling steps of recovery into a firm and solid life-
style walk. We do not have to be defeated.

Father, thank You for holding on to us on days
we want to run away.

Psalm 38

My wounds fester and are loathsome because of my
sinful folly. I am bowed down and brought very low;
all day long I go about mourning. My back is filled
with searing pain; there is no health in my body.
I am feeble and utterly crushed; I groan
in anguish of heart. (vv. 5-8)

Our bodies, souls, and spirits have been deeply
wounded by our addiction/codependency. The wounds
are infected and loathsome. Many inappropriate
behaviors are the result of these festering wounds.
Yes, this is the result of our own willful actions, our
sinful follies. This truth must be faced if recovery is
to progress. Along with the fact of our failures and
the resulting consequences, we must face still another
fact—that we have to forgive ourselves and stop
beating ourselves up. Until we have forgiven
ourselves, we will be depressed and angry, and that
will hinder the journey of recovery.

Addiction/codependency is a terminal illness unless
we begin to recover. At the beginning, we are feeble
and completely crushed. But our Father, with our
cooperation, can restore us to sanity.

Lord, please pour the healing oil of Your Spirit into
all that is wounded in us today.

Psalm 39

*I said, "I will watch my ways, and keep my tongue
from sin; I will put a muzzle on my mouth as long as
the wicked are in my presence." (v. 1)*

Most of us who are recovering have said the famous
"I can handle it." And we honestly thought we could.
After all, what could be so difficult about this
recovery business anyway? In our hands, our lives
are always out of control. That is so hard for most of
us to see, hear, admit, or even *think* about. Our lives
are so unstable that the thought of giving control to
another is frightening. But giving up control is the
first step to recovery; it is where recovery begins and
how recovery continues. It is a rude awakening when
we realize how finite our lives really are and how
little control we really do have. Our only hope is
God, someone we cannot see and usually cannot feel.
We must, by a choice of our wills, accept that He
really is and that He is the author of recovery.

*O God, help me remember that when I was in charge,
I made a mess.*

Psalm 40

I waited patiently for the Lord;
he turned to me and heard my cry. He lifted me
out of the slimy pit, out of the mud and mire;
he set my feet upon a rock and gave me a firm place
to stand. . . . I do not hide your righteousness
in my heart; I speak of your faithfulness and
salvation. I do not conceal your love and
your truth from the great assembly. (vv. 1-2; 10)

Addiction/codependency is a "slimy pit." In that pit is no good thing: no health, no joy, and no healthy relationship. In that slimy pit is nothing and no one who is stable. *Unmanageable* could be another word for that state. But God lifts us out. That would be enough; but notice that He goes a step further. He stabilizes and secures us. He takes us out of the quicksand life (addiction/codependency) and gives us a firm place to stand.

As recovery progresses, we do begin to sing a new song: it's the song of recovery. In Step Twelve, we take the message to others; and as we reach out to others, using our own story, others find the hope we have and begin to trust God for their recovery.

Taking the message to others keeps us active in our recovery. As we tell others about God's faithfulness in our journey of recovery, we hear it over and over. Every time we hear it, we are reminded of the hopeless state addiction/codependency had us in; we see God's goodness; and we encourage ourselves. Reaching out to others keeps recovery fresh.

Lord God, give me words that touch others and that encourage my own recovery.

Psalm 41

*Blessed is he who has regard for the weak; the Lord
delivers him in times of trouble.
The Lord will protect him and preserve his life;
He will bless him in the land and not
surrender Him to the desire of his foes.
The Lord will sustain him on his sickbed and restore
him from his bed of illness. I said, "O Lord, have
mercy on me; heal me, for I have sinned against
you." My enemies say of me in malice,
"When will he die and his name perish?". . .
All my enemies whisper together against me;
they imagine the worst for me, saying,
"A vile disease has beset him; he will never
get up from the place where he lies." (vv. 1-5; 7-8)*

The disease of addiction/codependency is vile. In our
weakness only God is able to deliver us from the
disease. God has protected us and has preserved our
lives many times. We and the disease together have
done everything possible to destroy ourselves. God
wants us whole, healed, delivered, and restored. This
is one of those times when sin requires healing along
with forgiveness.

Our enemies (addiction/codependency) are against us, against our recovery. God gives us hope when friends who do not understand discourage us and when the addiction/codependency tries to gain control. God will not let our enemies triumph over us.

Father, thank You for the promise of health and deliverance.

Psalm 42

*As the deer pants for streams of water, so my soul
pants for you, O God.
My soul thirsts for God, for the living God. When can
I go and meet with God? (vv. 1-2)*

Seldom do we realize that our innermost being longs
to be filled, but the longing is for far more than what
we find to fill it. It involves so much: our emptiness
from childhood, the pain of our addiction/codepend-
ency, and the frustration of recovery. Each thing is
felt strongly in our emotions. Our being is longing for
God. Our soul is thirsty for Him. Yet it seems almost
impossible that we would be able to approach Him, at
least our emotions tell us that, because we have
strayed from following Him. The memories of what
we have lost haunt us; we suffer depression over our
past. The only hope we have is to put our trust in
God. He is on our side even when we are not. We
often lash out at God, accusing Him of forgetting us.
We are convinced He has abandoned us. Today—in
spite of what our addiction/codependency tells us, in
spite of what our emotions say—we can choose to
hope in God.

*O God, fill all of my empty longings with Your Spirit
until I long no more.*

Psalm 43

*You are God my stronghold. Why have you rejected
me? Why must I go about mourning, oppressed
by the enemy? (v. 2)*

Many times, especially on those difficult days, it does
feel as though God has rejected us. It seems we are
left alone to battle through. Fear not; feelings never
tell us the facts but rather report what is going on
inside us. God promised not to leave us, though our
feelings say He has. But our wills decide. We can
choose to believe His Word, in spite of what we feel.
He has told us the truth.

Mourning and grieving are important aspects of
recovery. Grief is often a normal and healthy stage of
recovery. On the other hand, the "pity pot" is that
destructive "why me?" attitude that slows down our
recovery.

We should allow ourselves to grieve but not to be
consumed by grief. We may let it be a part of the
journey but not the destination.

*Father, help me to know the difference between
grieving and sitting on the "pity pot."*

Psalm 44

It was not by their sword that they won the land, nor did their arm bring them victory; it was your right hand, your arm, and the light of your face, for you loved them. . . . Awake, O Lord! Why do you sleep? Rouse yourself! Do not reject us forever. (vv. 3; 23)

Self-work will not free us from our addiction. But is not that what the First Step is really saying? Nothing we can do, nothing we have done has brought us freedom.

Turning over a million new leaves, a million broken promises, and a million shattered plans—not once did any of that help. It is only when we are convinced that we have *no power* or ability over our addiction/codependency and we turn our lives over to God is there hope for victory. He gives us this victory because He loves us.

Yet, at times we've accused God of taking a nap, especially when our recovery is not going as we had planned. Oops! There's the catch; we keep forgetting who is in charge.

Father, I give You the life I have been unable to manage. I resign!

Psalm 45

*In your majesty ride forth victoriously in behalf of
truth, humility and righteousness;
let your right hand display awesome deeds. (v. 4)*

Victory comes in our recovery as the result of truth,
humility, and righteousness. Truth brought us out of
denial; we admitted we were powerless. We made a
decision to turn our lives and will over to the care of
God. We made a fearless, searching moral inventory.
Then we made a list of all the people we had
wronged and became willing to make direct amends.
Now we continue to take a personal inventory and,
when wrong, promptly admit it.

These steps help us become humble. Who can look
honestly at the messes we've made and remain
proud? In humility, we made a decision to turn our
lives and wills over to God. Righteousness cannot be
attained by our own works but is a gift that is ours as
a result of Steps Two through Eleven. It is the fruit of
recovery.

*Lord, some days I want to hide from life. Give me
courage to face reality.*

Psalm 46

God is our refuge and strength,
an ever-present help in trouble. Therefore
we will not fear, though the earth give way and
the mountains fall into the heart of the sea, though
its surging. . . . Be still, and know that I am God;
I will be exalted among the nations,
I will be exalted in the earth. (vv. 1-3; 10)

It can become a great comfort to our trembling, fearful heart to know that God wants to be a refuge and strength, a constant help when we are in trouble—especially when the trouble is the result of our foolish living and wrong choices.

Even when we find ourselves in the midst of a personal earthquake, we can rest in His promise to keep us safe. We can know that there is a river of safety, a place of security, hidden away in the safety of God. God is our fortress, our safe place, our comfortable place. When we've stood all the pain we can, when we feel like a lost, frightened child, when we are confused and hurt, we can run to the safety of God's arms.

Stop! Be still! Look! Look at the lives of those who are successful in their journeys of recovery. Look, see how much peace replaced that inner turmoil. *Be still and know:* be still and meditate on Him.

O God, develop in me the ability to trust in Your power to see me through the earthquakes in my life.

Psalm 47

Clap your hands, all you nations; shout to God with cries of joy. (v. 1)

On the days when we feel well and the family isn't in turmoil, it is easy to clap our hands and shout to God with cries of joy. And just as there are bad days, there are good days in recovery. Perhaps today is not a good one, and to praise God seems ludicrous. Many times recovery requires us to stretch beyond the comfortable: to step when we'd rather sit, to praise when we'd rather whine or grumble. But to praise in the midst of our trouble, pain, or discouragement is a sacrifice of praise. To speak positive words even when we don't feel them, begins a change in our emotions. So even if this is not a day that would ordinarily evoke praise, why not, by an act of our wills, begin to praise God? For what? Look at where we have been, where we are today, and where we are heading. Now look at where we were and the direction we'd be going if God had not reached into the pit to rescue us. Is that not worth a few shouts of praise?

O God, give me a voice to praise You in the midst of my brokenness.

Psalm 48

Within your temple, O God, we meditate on
your unfailing love. . . . For this God is our
God for ever and ever; he will be our guide
even to the end. (vv. 9; 14)

To meditate requires discipline that few of us possess at the beginning of our recovery. Maybe that is why this is Step Eleven and not Step Three. To meditate means to stop, to sit long enough in God's presence to quiet the rushing thoughts, and to center (lock in) on a God who loves us unconditionally. To do this brings stability into our lives that we have not had before. To renew our minds from the old thinking—that God is absent, angry, or hates us—to correct thinking about His *unfailing love* brings a peace that we need in order to continue our recovery. To meditate means to keep mulling over and over, to remind ourselves continually of God's love and care.

God is the only one who is able and who is willing to guide us out of the mess we've found ourselves in through our addiction/codependency.

Lord, I've never learned to be still and know You.
Teach me now, please.

Psalm 49

My mouth will speak words of wisdom; the
utterance from my heart will give understanding. . . .
Why should I fear when evil days come, when wicked
deceivers surround me. . . . No man can redeem the
life of another or give God a ransom for him. . . .
But God will redeem my life from the grave;
he will surely take me to himself. (vv. 3; 5; 7; 15)

Listen to the unrehearsed words that come
"unbidden" from the inner being. If we watch reactions that come spontaneously, we will have an
understanding of the way things really are deep
inside. Our reactions expose the real us. Part of Step
Ten is to continue to take a personal inventory. To
evaluate our unplanned reactions will help us do this.

Bad days will come during our recovery. Some days
we will want to give up. Some days it will seem we
have lost all the ground we had gained. Temporary
setbacks are just that, temporary. Don't be fooled;
don't stop; don't quit! Get back up, re-gather your
resources, and move on.

Caretakers have the mistaken idea that they can love or give or do enough to make the addict well. Many become codependent because of this false belief. However, God will redeem our lives from destruction. He will deliver us. He will teach us how to live.

*Lord, give me strength to get up one more
time than I fall.*

Psalm 50

*"Gather to me my consecrated ones, who made a
covenant with me by sacrifice."
And the heavens proclaim his righteousness, for God
himself is judge. (vv. 5-6)*

Every word of this Psalm seems to scorch, yet each
one is true of our addictive/codependent nature. Our
addictive/codependent nature is selfish, self-gratify-
ing, and will stop at nothing to satisfy the craving. It
would have us lie, manipulate, cheat, control, or
bargain. These practices in our old nature do not
cease just because we decide to recover; they must be
brought to death daily through a moral inventory.
Facing ourselves is difficult to do but is certainly a
big and important daily step.

*Father, aid me as I search out the inner
depths of my heart.*

Psalm 51

*Have mercy on me, O God, according to your
unfailing love; according to your great
compassion blot out my transgressions.
Wash away all my iniquity and cleanse me from my
sin. For I know my transgression, and
my sin is always before me. . . . Surely you desire
truth in the inner parts; you teach me wisdom
in the inmost place. Cleanse me with hyssop,
and I will be clean; wash me, and I will be whiter
than snow. . . . . Hide your face from my sins and blot
out all my iniquity. . . . Restore to me the joy of your
salvation and grant me a willing spirit, to sustain me.
Then I will teach transgressors your ways, and
sinners will turn back to you. . . . The sacrifices of
God are a broken spirit; a broken and
contrite heart, O God, you will not despise.
(vv. 1-3; 6-7; 9; 12-13; 17)*

One way of admitting that we are powerless would be
to ask God to have mercy on us. "Wash away all my
iniquity and cleanse me from my sin" is certainly a
verbal declaration of our faith that God can restore
us. Asking Him to forgive and help us begins the
process of turning our lives and wills over to God.
David certainly made a fearless, searching, moral
inventory of his life as he realized his transgressions
and was quick to admit to God and to himself what a

mess he was in. We have to get there, too. We are ready to have God remove these defects when we say along with David, "Hide Your face from my sins and blot out all my iniquity." After our spiritual awakening, we do want to tell fellow strugglers that it is possible to be free. What a beautiful summation of the Twelve Steps David gives us in this Psalm!

God, I need Your help in working these Steps rather than taking a shortcut.

Psalm 52

Why do you boast of evil, you mighty man?
Why do you boast all day long, you who are
a disgrace in the eyes of God?. . .
"Here now is the man who did not make God his
stronghold but trusted in his great wealth
and grew strong by destroying others!" But I am like
an olive tree flourishing in the house of God;
I trust in God's unfailing love for ever and ever.
I will praise you forever for what you have done;
in your name I will hope, for your name is good.
I will praise you in the presence of your saints.
(vv. 1; 7-9)

Boasting is a symptom of poor self-esteem and low self-worth. Being addicts/codependents, our self-concepts are usually not very good. One unhealthy and non-productive way of handling poor self-esteem is to brag. But look at the end of boasting: Our tongues cannot save us, change us, or deliver us from a poor self-image; they will only cover up. Speaking the truth about ourselves is so difficult; it hurts too badly to see who we really are. God desires to destroy that false self-image so that it will stop producing sour fruit in our lives. Boasting ends with us still trusting in something we do that makes us feel a little better; it may also include putting others down and belittling them. Trusting in self is disastrous.

But, when we do trust in what God says about us, we realize He has spoken of our worth as a person by His sacrifice for us.

God, give me eyes to see myself the way You do and to voice Your truth instead of boasting.

Psalm 53

There they were, overwhelmed with dread,
where there was nothing to dread.
God scattered the bones of those who
attacked you; you put them to shame,
for God despised them. (v. 5)

Often in our recovery, we are overwhelmed with dread. Our feelings are waking up, and we are more in touch with the negative emotions. We are full of dread, full of "what ifs" and full of "should have's." But we cannot deal with the abstracts; we can only deal with reality. Dread is the emotion that steals the joy from everyday living and hinders our journey of recovery.

Whatever our reality is today, God gives us strength and courage to face it and overcome it. Much of what we fear never happens, and we spend endless energy trying to deal with imaginary possibilities.

Father, teach me how to lay aside the "what if's"
and "should have's" and face life realistically.

Psalm 54

*Strangers are attacking me; ruthless men seek my
life—men without regard for God.
Surely God is my help; the Lord is the one who
sustains me. . . . For he has delivered me from
all my troubles, and my eyes have looked
in triumph on my foes. (vv. 3-4; 7)*

Our battle is not with human beings—our battle is
with our own stinking thinking, our own inability and
unwillingness to let go and let God. We must release
our desire to control and manipulate. That frees us to
do battle against the *real enemy*. God is willing to
deliver us from all the troubles we have encountered
as a result of our addiction/codependency. But it is
not an instant, quick fix, a guaranteed no-pain way to
happiness. It happens as we are faithful to our program. Working those Steps daily, recovery happens
"here a little, there a little," in twenty-four-hours-a-
day, one-day-at-a-time segments.

*Lord, sometimes I'd like to skip over the mundane
Steps of recovery. Help me stick to the
Steps faithfully.*

Psalm 55

Listen to my prayer, O God, do not ignore my plea;
hear me and answer me. My thoughts trouble me and
I am distraught at the voice of the enemy, at the
stares of the wicked; for they bring down suffering
upon me and revile me in their anger. (vv. 1-3)

On some days, we feel that God is probably sick of hearing from us. Like parents who tire of answering a child's endless "why's," it feels like He is ignoring us.

Once more, we have fallen prey to crazy thinking, and we are relying on our emotions for the truth. Stinking thinking does trouble us, because those thoughts do not go in the same direction as our recovery is going. Indeed, our heart is in anguish; we have not left behind a drink, drug, or relationship, but a life-style. At times we may feel we will die, and yet we are afraid we won't die. It's natural to want to run away and hide, but this problem of addiction/codependency can't be run from; it must be conquered. Even in that, we have to go back to our own personal powerlessness and God's ability to restore us to sanity.

Lord, what a humbling experience to realize that I
need Your help in conquering this disease.

Psalm 56

*My slanderers pursue me all day long; many are
attacking me in their pride. (v. 2)*

Our slanderers are not powerful outside forces; the
real slanderers come from our own self-talk. There is
the real problem. Self-esteem and self-worth respond
to what we say to ourselves about ourselves, about
our recovery, about life, and about God. Whatever we
tell ourselves affects the way we view and feel about
ourselves.

We also give others the power to determine how we
view ourselves as people. When these others affirm
us, we feel good about ourselves; when they withhold
positive comments or responses, we feel bad. We
may then work even harder to get the response we
want. The one positive response we need most is not
our spouse's, friends', parents', or employer's—it is
our own!

So why not begin to say some good things to yourself
about "yours truly?"

*Father, teach me to embrace what You say,
especially when it isn't what I want to hear.*

Psalm 57

*Have mercy on me, O God, have mercy on me, for in
you my soul takes refuge. I will take refuge in the
shadow of your wings until the disaster has passed.
I cry out to God Most High, to God, who fulfills his
purpose for me. (vv. 1-2)*

Often our self-esteem is so low because of the big
mess we made during the days before recovery.
Therefore, it is difficult to remember that God's
mercy never ends. We cannot exhaust it! Maybe we
have a tendency to think (feel) about God's mercy in
the same way we extend mercy to others. But our
God is the expert on mercy; He always has more than
enough. Most of us have a tendency to take refuge in
God as long as the storm lasts or the disaster lasts;
but we get into trouble when we venture out of the
safety of totally depending on Him.

Anytime the pain becomes too intense, we can cry
out to God, who has a purpose for us and who is
faithful to fulfill it, if we cooperate. We may lose
sight of His plan or purpose, but He never does. On
our most bewildering, confusing days He knows
where we are going and how to get us there.

*O God, help me to accept the mercy that You
constantly extend to me.*

Psalm 58

Do you rulers indeed speak justly?
Do you judge uprightly among men?
No, in your heart you devise injustice,
and your hands mete out
violence on the earth.
Even from birth the wicked go astray,
from the womb they
are wayward and speak lies. (vv. 1-3)

In our own hearts, we are very hard on ourselves. We are not fair; we are not just. We strike out at ourselves with cruel words, hateful remarks, and behaviors that punish. From some of our earliest memories comes the feeling that we are worthless. What rules our recovery? Who is king over the enemy of addiction/codependency when we think we are in charge? When we fail to work our program? When we forget that we are absolutely powerless over addiction/codependency? If we follow our own hearts, we will fail.

Our best efforts will not carry us through as addicts/codependents; it is a most difficult thing to place trust in someone other than ourselves. Giving control to someone else is frightening because for so long our lives have been out of control while we thought we were in control. God our Father is the only one able to bring control, as we allow Him to rule as King in our recovery.

Father, today I resign as king, and I appoint You to rule my recovery.

Psalm 59

Deliver me from my enemies, O God; protect me from those who rise up against me. (v. 1)

Many times our addiction/codependency began because of painful emotions we had tried to cover up or numb out. Therefore, we now see emotions as the enemy; we run from pain. Guilt, shame, failure, and confusion all work together to keep us from recovering. That little wounded child inside us is so ashamed because he or she seems to be so bad. For many of us, there was no emotionally whole parent who could help dispel our fears about life and help us see that we were not responsible for someone else's pain.

In recovery, we must make peace with that little wounded child of our past, allowing God to be that parent who loves and nurtures. We must face the hurtful events and emotions of the past and once and for all deal with and cut free from yesterday to face the possibility of recovery today.

O God, please cut me free from yesterday through resolving those hurtful issues.

Psalm 60

You have rejected us, O God, and burst forth upon
us; you have been angry—now
restore us! You have shaken the land and torn it
open; mend its fractures, for it is quaking. . . . Give
us aid against the enemy, for the help of man is
worthless. With God we will gain the victory, and he
will trample down our enemies. (vv. 1-2; 11-12)

The still "un-recovering" part of us speaks the fear, doubt, and unbelief that we hold in our hearts. That unhealthy part fears that God has rejected us and has abused us and is angry with us. But we continue to cry out for restoration with that part of us that is healthy.

Our unhealthy part continues its stinking thinking, feeling that it is God who has shaken us and torn our lives open. The recovering part of us knows that it is only God who can set us free, that even in the midst of our addiction, He does love us.

Oftentimes we accuse God of leaving us, but actually we are the ones who distanced ourselves from God, possibly because of our shame and feelings of guilt over our past.

Yet recovery continues when we realize once more that He is the only one who can truly set us free. Only God can trample down the enemy of addition/co-dependence.

Father, please remind me that You are near, regardless of what my emotions tell me.

Psalm 61

*Hear my cry, O God; listen to my prayer. From the
ends of the earth I call to you, I call
as my heart grows faint; lead me to the rock
that is higher than I. For you have been my refuge,
a strong tower against the foe. I long to dwell
in your tent forever and take refuge
in the shelter of your wings. (vv. 1-4)*

While our spirits long for communion with God, our
flesh struggles against it. Our flesh, as always, wants
to be in control, wants to be gratified. Most of us did
not call on God until we had grown so faint that we
knew we were going to die. We cried out only when
we realized that we were truly powerless over our
addiction/codependency.

But in our faint condition, it is good to know that
there is a rock that is stronger than we have ever
been. It is that rock that is our refuge, our strong
tower, and our shelter. Our rock is always open for
us. This becomes more and more evident as we
recover and practice coming to Him and finding He is
there.

*Father, help me to accept my weakness as a gift that
directs me to Your strength.*

Psalm 62

*My soul finds rest in God alone; my salvation comes
from him. He alone is my rock and my salvation; he
is my fortress, I will never be shaken. (vv. 1-2)*

" . . . in God alone." What a sobering thought and yet
how true. Our salvation comes from God; deliverance
comes from God; recovery comes from God. Our
souls can rest in God alone. He alone is our rock,
salvation, and fortress. Even our worth as people is
determined by God alone; and as we turn to Him, He
reminds us that He loves us as we are.

Only as we daily walk in the Twelve Steps, reminding ourselves that God alone is able to truly change
us, can we know that we will not be shaken. Only as
we submit to His leadership and obey His instruction
can we be assured of success in our journey to
recovery.

God alone plus one willing person equals recovery
today.

*Lord, help me join forces with Your plan of recovery
for my life.*

Psalm 63

O God, you are my God, earnestly I seek you;
my soul thirst for you, my body longs for
you, in a dry and weary land where there
is no water. . . . I will praise you as long
as I live, and in your name I will lift up
my hands. . . . On my bed I remember you;
I think of you through the watches of the
night. . . . My soul clings to you; your
right hand upholds me. (vv. 1; 4; 6; 8)

What a beautiful description of Steps Two, Three, Eleven, and Twelve. Convinced that we can reach out to God, we begin to seeking Him earnestly, longing for Him, thirsting for Him. Our lives were so dry and so empty; at last we began to come to an awareness that He was waiting to fill that which was empty, and to satisfy that which was longing.

Many a nights' sleep escapes us as we go over and over things we cannot change, but what a difference those sleepless nights can bring if we begin instead to meditate on God, who is the author and finisher of our recovery. Often as addicts and codependents, we want to cling to someone or something; but as we improve our knowledge and understanding of God, we learn to cling to Him. How tightly He holds us to

His bosom as we draw from Him the strength to face a new day of recovery.

O Lord, give me strength to turn to You,
the author and finisher of my recovery.

Psalm 66

*Come and see what God has done, how awesome his
works in man's behalf! . . . he has preserved
our lives and kept our feet from slipping. . . . I will
come to your temple with burnt offerings and fulfill
my vows to you. . . . Praise be to God, who
has not rejected my prayer or withheld
his love from me! (vv. 5; 9; 13; 20)*

When we look at where we were *before* recovery and
compare it to where we are *now*, we'll know for sure
that God was the only one who could do it! In our
lives as recovering addicts/codependents, we know
that His deeds are awesome, His power is great. So
often He has preserved our lives, even when we were
ready for a major fall. He helped us find a better way.

One of our behaviors as addicts/codependents is to
blame others, blame anyone and everyone for
anything and everything. We even try to blame God.
But even so, He brings us to a place of abundance
(v.12).

In the bargaining stage of recovery, we often make promises to God. Some we need to keep, but others we need to lay aside for what they were: words of bargaining that resulted from the pain we were feeling.

God never withholds His love from us; but often the pain is so intense, we may not feel His love and care. Still, He is there, loving us back to life.

O God, constantly remind me of the place from which You have brought me.

Psalm 67

May God be gracious to us and bless us and make his face shine upon us; that your ways may be known on earth, your salvation among all nations. (vv. 1-2)

A grateful heart is always in order; but for those who are in pain, or in the earlier stages of recovery, it may be difficult to thank or praise. But even in our brokenness, praise is good.

Praise brings the presence of God into our situation; praise is a positive force against negative happenings and the resulting emotions. Praise is verbally expressing what God has done in our lives. Praise is one way of getting the message to others when we are working the Twelve Steps.

Why not replace grumbling with praise and see if there isn't much more joy and peace inside our hearts?

Father, help praise come from my lips, especially at the times I'd rather complain.

Psalm 68

A father to the fatherless, a defender of widows,
is God in his holy dwelling. God sets the lonely
in families, he leads forth the prisoners with
singing; but the rebellious live in a
sun-scorched land. (vv. 5-6)

Many of us who are recovering were raised in alcoholic, dysfunctional, or neurotic families. As a result, we may have felt as if we were the parent. We had little emotional support, little nurture, because one parent was dysfunctional and the other parent was codependent, taking care of and trying to control the other parent's behavior. So that left us as children to try to figure life out. But in recovery, God will Himself parent us and teach us how to be a parent to that little wounded child inside. God places us in spiritual families (local fellowships) to further our growth. Whether it is our church family or support group, they become our family in recovery.

Lord, help me to learn that You are
the only perfect parent.

Psalm 69

*Save me, O God, for the waters have come up to
my neck. I sink in the miry depths, where there
is no foothold. I have come into the deep waters;
the floods engulf me. I am worn out calling for help;
my throat is parched. My eyes fail, looking for
my God. . . . You know my folly, O God; my guilt is
not hidden from you. . . . I am a stranger to
my brothers, an alien to my own mother's sons.
(vv. 1-3; 5; 8)*

We are reminded in Steps Eight and Nine that
sobriety brings with it a new dimension: facing what
we have not faced before, feeling those emotions that
have been stuffed down and denied. When this
happens it *does* feel as if the waters are going to
overwhelm us.

Addiction steals from us, but we have to pay the price
for what has been stolen. Many times restitution is
only the beginning of the price we must pay.

God indeed knows our folly; He is aware of our guilt, and yet, He still wants us. Only God understands us completely, and only He can free us. Our addiction/codependency destroys our ability to have intimate relationships with anyone. But as we are faithful to work that Eighth and Ninth Step, God is able to use this most humbling experience to build bridges over the wide gulf between us and those we have hurt.

God, sometimes it seems that my emotions are too much. Help me process them and let them go.

Psalm 70

Hasten, O God, save me; O Lord, come quickly to help me. . . .Yet I am poor and needy; come quickly to me, O God. You are my help and my deliverer; O Lord, do not delay. (vv. 1; 5)

Instant healing—we all wish for it. But like many instant foods, there seems to be something missing. God works in our lives in times and seasons, and we don't have to remind Him how badly we hurt or how long we have suffered. We don't even have to refresh His memory on how desperately we want to be whole. If there seems to be a delay, there is a reason. Many of the lessons we learn in patience will bless us later. When we are poor and needy, we do want a quick fix. Hurry, hurry, hurry and make this pain stop. Isn't that how we got into our addiction/codependency in the first place? So we need to

- slow down,
- stop chomping at the bit,
- wait,
- remember.

God is the one in charge of our recovery, and He knows exactly how to direct us so that we recover on a daily basis.

Lord, teach me to rest when there is a delay.

Psalm 71

*In you, O Lord, I haven taken refuge; let me never be
put to shame. . . . For you have been my hope, O
Sovereign Lord, my confidence since my youth.
From birth I have relied on you; you brought me
forth from my mother's womb. I will ever praise you.
. . . Do not cast me away when I am old; do not
forsake me when my strength is gone. (vv. 1; 5-6; 9)*

When we make a decision to turn our lives and wills
over to God, we are able to take refuge in the Lord.
Only then can there be any continuing wholeness. We
have learned in our Step One living that whatever is
done in our own strength is as fickle as the wind. Our
strength fails all too quickly.

Hope—what a wonderful word and what an attitude
toward God! He is our hope of recovery. He is our
confidence for the future.

When we have strength, we are going to fall back
into "I can handle it," so it is a blessing if we have no
strength. We can be assured that He will not forsake
us even at our weakest moments. The most important
emotion in recovery is hope.

*Lord, I ask You to restore my ability to hope,
especially when I feel hopeless.*

Psalm 72

He will defend the afflicted among the people and save the children of the needy. . . . For he will deliver the needy who cry out, the afflicted who have no one to help. He will take pity on the weak and the needy and save the needy from death. He will rescue them from oppression and violence, for precious is their blood in his sight.(vv. 4; 12-14)

The words *afflicted, needy,* and *weak,* which appear in these verses—what a description of our powerlessness and unmanageable lives before recovery. *Defend, save, deliver,* and *rescue* are the words that describe the results of turning our lives and wills over to God in recovery.

God is on our side; He is not against us. What a comfort to begin to learn this. As addicted/codependent people, we have hated ourselves so much that it is a comfort to realize that God does not hate us. God wants to deliver us, the afflicted, needy, and weak. He will strengthen that which is weak; He will fulfill that which is needy and deliver us from the affliction of addiction/codependency.

Lord, You are on my side. Help me to be on my side, too.

Psalm 73

*For I envied the arrogant when I saw the prosperity
of the wicked. They have no struggles; their bodies
are healthy and strong. . . . This is what the wicked
are like—always carefree, they increase in wealth.
Surely in vain have I kept my heart pure; in vain have
I washed my hands in innocence. (vv. 3-4; 12-13)*

Continuing a *personal* inventory will keep us busy.
Getting our eyes on others is always a poor choice.
Trying to work someone else's program will cause us
to get bogged down. It is easy to get resentful
towards those who *seem* to be free and those who
have not suffered as we have.

It seems. . . . It feels. . . . We assume. . . . These three
statements get recovering people into trouble every
time. Look at verse 12: The wicked *seem* to be
"always carefree [and increasing] in wealth." It *feels*
that we have kept our hearts pure in vain. We *assume*
that this is the way it is.

Sometimes in our pain we are angry with God, and
yet He holds onto us and guides us. Our strength will
fail, but God's strength will not fail. It is good to be
near God.

*O God, help me to be honest about my inventory and
faithful to work my program.*

Psalm 74

Your foes roared in the place where you met with us;
they set up their standards as signs. They behaved
like men wielding axes to cut through a thicket of
trees. They smashed all the carved paneling with
their axes and hatchets. They burned your sanctuary
to the ground; they defied the dwelling place of your
Name. They said in their heart, "We will crush them
completely!" They burned every place where
God was worshiped in the land. (vv. 4-8)

Not only is our addiction/codependency our enemy, but it is also God's enemy because it steals us from Him. We are bound with iron fetters to something as insignificant as a drink . . . a drug . . . a circumstance . . . a relationship . . . an activity—something that will consume and control us.

Addiction/codependency mocks us! How simple it would be for God to take his hand and wipe out the disease, yet He doesn't do it that way. It is a tiny step here, another step there, a larger step somewhere else. It is a new attitude: learning to rest instead of struggle. It is growth in Him: coming to know that only God can set us free as we cooperate with Him on a daily basis.

Lord, help me to be grateful for the daily and
seemingly insignificant steps of recovery.

Psalm 75

You say, "I choose the appointed time; it is I who judge uprightly." (v. 2)

"The appointed time"—yet much of our frustrations in recovery come from our trying to push and pull, trying to force recovery at a faster pace. We all want too much too soon, but that buildup can cause us to relapse. Babies grow and develop at their own pace, and all the bragging mamas in the world can't circumvent their baby's progress. Sometimes children miss a step or stage of development, and they have other problems later on. So it is with our recovery. One Step builds upon another; one Step compliments the former Step. Step One without Step Two is worthless. Steps are just that—steps. Each addict/codependent is an individual. He or she is a unique, one-of-a-kind designer's original. Each person recovers at his or her own speed. Our "appointed time" includes where we are today. Not one Step is wasted; each is important. God's timetable is usually quite different from ours, but His is always "right on schedule."

God, help me not to balk but to walk, step by step.

Psalm 76

*When you, O God, rose up to judge, to save
all the afflicted of the land. . . .
He breaks the spirit of rulers; he is feared
by the kings of the earth. (vv. 9; 12)*

Surely no afflictions affect more people than
addiction and codependency. Millions of people are
affected in some way. Either they are addicts, they
live with an addict, or they were raised by an addict.
Addiction has indeed ruled our lives and controlled
our emotions, and we have struggled to get free or to
get others free. Only God is able to break the spirit of
the addiction that has been the ruler of our lives.

If we try to rule, we are controlled; if we allow God
to rule, we are free. So it's an easy choice to make, or
at least it should be.

God, give me grace to resign and allow You to rule.

Psalm 77

I cried to God for help; I cried out to God to hear me.
When I was in distress, I sought the Lord;
at night I stretched out untiring hands and my
soul refused to be comforted. (vv. 1-2)

Sad to say, but for most of us, only distress in our addicted/codependent circumstances will bring us to the place of recovery. Some days during our recovery are intense with pain. It may be

- spiritual
- relational
- emotional
- physical
- financial

The pain may cause tears, praying, and crying out for help. When we experience pain, it may register as God's anger or His punishment, but not so. It is God's mercy, even "severe mercy," which brings us to the end of ourselves. The pain and difficulty then become not a negative but a positive thing, because it brought us to a life-changing, full-of-hope pathway into recovery. Don't waste pain; look for a doorway into new areas of recovery.

Lord, I thank You for the distress that
brought me to recovery.

Psalm 78

*. . . what we have heard and know, what our fathers
have told us. We will not hide them from their
children; we will tell the next generation the
praiseworthy deeds of the Lord, his power, and the
wonders he has done. (vv. 3-4)*

This entire Psalm is the history of God's faithfulness
to His rebellious, hard-headed, stubborn children. In
reading this Psalm, we find not only God's anger and
correction, but also His miracles performed over and
over. But most of all, we see His faithfulness—*in
spite of how the "kids" acted*. These stories were to
be passed on from generation to generation and from
family to family.

 Likewise, our stories of recovery should be passed
on to others who are still struggling and have not
chosen the way of recovery, as well as to those who
are well into recovery. Names, dates, and places are
different, but the up-and-down struggle is very
similar. We are encouraged when we hear of
someone else who felt what we are feeling and has
now experienced victory.

Sharing our Step Twelve, the "good news" that God loves addicts/codependents and has a plan to get us free, gives hope to those who are still struggling.

We also need to share our stories with our children because we know that addiction/codependency is a disease passed on to the next generation. The principles of recovery can also be passed along in just the same way.

Father, let my story of recovery make others
aware of Your faithfulness.

Psalm 79

*Help us, O God our Savior, for the glory of your
name; deliver us and forgive our sins
for your name's sake. . . . Then we your people, the
sheep of your pasture, will praise you forever; from
generation to generation we will recount your praise.*
(vv. 9; 13)

To admit to God, ourselves, and to another human
that we are wrong is a real pride killer. As difficult as
it is to come to that place, it is even more difficult to
allow God to remove these defects. Yet our desperate
need makes us ready.

To know that we need surgery is sobering. But to
actually be wheeled down the hall, have the IV
inserted, and wait for the anesthesia to put us under is
a new ball game altogether. Waking up to the post-
surgical pain, however, is hardest of all.

Allowing God to remove these defects of character would be no problem at all if He could just instantly wave His hand and the defects would be gone. But He is removing diseased habit-structures, and this soul surgery is painful. The promise is that, when we have recovered, we will have the ability to live life without being bogged down with the excess luggage. We will praise God and be joyful; we can share the story of recovery with others who travel along this same pathway.

*Father, give me strength of spirit
to endure the healing pain.*

Psalm 80

*Restore us, O God; make your face shine upon us
that we may be saved. . . . Then we will not turn away
from you; revive us, and we will call on your name.*
(vv. 3; 18)

The theme of recovery is restoration. Addiction/co-
dependency is the destroyer, the stealer, the author of
ruined lives, families, and people. What a blessing to
realize that God can and will restore and revive.

"Restore us, O God" is the prayer of recovery; not
"fix" us, not merely stop the pain, but rather restore
and remake us. Remodel our thinking, our mindset;
renew our spirit, and rekindle our zest for living. That
is a prayer that our Father delights in answering.

In recovery, the problem is never with God but with
our unreal expectations of how and when this
restoration should take place. Restoration is not a
quick, prefabricated project that is thrown together. It
is a deliberate and planned removal of the unwanted,
a detailed refining of that which is to be preserved,
and an addition of that which was not before.
Restoration in recovery is similar: removing defects
of character, correcting stinking thinking, and giving
us hope we've never experienced.

*Lord, teach me to wait for restoration when my
impatience is crying for a quick fix.*

Psalm 81

But my people would not listen to me;
Israel would not submit to me. So I gave them
over to their stubborn hearts to follow their own
devices. If my people would but listen to me, if Israel
would follow my ways, how quickly would I
subdue their enemies and turn my hand against
their foes! (vv. 11-14)

It is a major accomplishment to turn our wills over to God. We are stubborn people, and we want things our way, even recovery. One of our downfalls in recovery is that we resist listening to God. The voice of our enemy—our voice, the voice of defeat—we will hear; but we have trouble listening to God. Could that be because His voice speaks hope, and we feel hopeless? His voice speaks reality, and we live in denial? His voice corrects, and we don't want to change? His voice also tells us who we really are, and His voice reminds us that He sees us differently than others view us. Recovery would progress much quicker if only we would listen to God. When we listen to God, we learn to follow His ways, and that brings our enemy of addiction/codependency to an abrupt end. Let's stop and listen to our Father today and allow His Words to encourage and strengthen us.

O God, train my ears to hear Your voice.

Psalm 82

Defend the cause of the weak
and fatherless; maintain the rights
of the poor and oppressed.
Rescue the weak and needy;
deliver them from the hand of the wicked.
They know nothing, they understand nothing.
They walk about in darkness;
all the foundations of the earth are shaken. (vv. 3-5)

Many addicts/codependents were raised in dysfunctional or alcoholic homes. Adult children of alcoholic/dysfunctional families are still little children inside. Weak and fatherless, we became poor, oppressed, and very needy. Most of us seek some way besides God to fill this need, and thus we have delivered ourselves into the control of addiction/codependency ("the wicked"). Our Father will deliver us from the hand of the wicked if we will only come to Him.

It is a very humbling experience to realize that we are in control of only one thing—admitting that we are powerless. Yet in that admission, we place ourselves in a position to be a child with our Father and to have our previously unmet needs met. As the little wounded child within is nurtured and becomes whole, the adult begins to walk consistently in recovery. God delights in our being a child with Him.

Father, help me to place myself in the position of being Your child today.

Psalm 83

O God, do not keep silent; be not quiet,
O God, be not still. (v. 1)

Many times we want to help our Father "hurry up." We want to be on God's vengeance team; and most certainly, we want to tell Him how to do things. Is that still our addictive/codependent nature trying to be in control, even of God? For so long in our codependency we have tried to run the show by telling others what they should or should not do. From time to time, we forget that we can't even run our own lives. How ludicrous that we who have made such a mess of everything in our lives would think that we could help even one person straighten out his or her situation. But, oh, how we try.

God knows how to run His universe; He knows who needs what and exactly when certain things need to happen.

So what can we do? Turn our lives and wills over to God and resign our positions as assistants to God.

Lord, are You absolutely sure that
You can handle my recovery?

Psalm 84

My soul yearns, even faints, for the courts
of the Lord; my heart and my flesh
cry out for the living God. . . . As they
pass through the Valley of Baca,
they make it a place of springs;
the autumn rains also cover it with pools.
They go from strength to strength,
till each appears before God in Zion. (vv. 2; 6-7)

It seems that tears can wash away years of poison, cleansing the soul and preparing us for growth. As addicts/codependents, we were stuck for so long in the pity-party syndrome that, even though we may have cried, the tears were not really healing tears.

In recovery, we will pass through many valleys of tears. Be it tears of frustration, anger, grief, loneliness, or separation, they can become tears of healing if, in the midst of our pain, we cry out for the living God to change us.

In recovery, we experience so many emotions, from deep sorrow to excitement and joy. Before recovery, we had anesthetized our ability to feel because most of what we felt was negative and brought pain. But we can't turn off negative emotions without turning off the positive emotions. As Christians in recovery, we may think it's wrong to feel this or that; but we feel what we feel. How we handle these emotions is what makes them right or wrong. Notice that we are to "pass through" the place of tears—not build a house and live there. Our Father created us as emotional beings, and He can teach us how to handle and express human emotions in a healthy way.

O God, teach me to weep the tears
that aid my recovery.

Psalm 85

*Show us your unfailing love, O Lord, and grant us
your salvation. . . . Love and faithfulness meet
together, righteousness and peace kiss each other.
Faithfulness springs forth from the earth, and
righteousness looks down from heaven.
The Lord will indeed give what is good, and our land
will yield its harvest. (vv. 7; 10-12)*

Recovery progresses as our sponsors, loved ones, and friends exhibit "tough love." Often God will love us with that non-compromising love that will not allow us to become sloppy in our recovery. It isn't because He is angry with us but because He knows how easily we excuse the flesh, and how recovery is slowed down when we feed our old nature. Our Father wants us to be free. Therefore, when we begin self-defeating behaviors, His love confronts us. God's love, though tough, is unfailing even in the midst of our worst pain, the most insane craziness that we exhibited in addiction/codependency, and even in the middle of denial.

His love is His faithfulness demonstrated to us in many ways. One of these is His commitment to our recovery.

*Father, help me accept Your
gift of unconditional love.*

Psalm 86

*Teach me your way, O Lord, and I will
walk in your truth; give me an undivided heart,
that I may fear your name. (v. 11)*

In recovery, some tasks God only can perform; others, we together accomplish, and a few are ours alone. God cannot do our job of cooperating with the program. Only we can work the Twelve Steps, but God alone can give us an undivided heart.

As addicts/codependents, we have a divided heart that *always* reaches for something or someone who will temporarily cause us to feel better. We get into relationships or into other addictions thinking these will bring happiness. Only as we become aware that we cannot unite our own hearts and as we come to the Mender of Broken Hearts, will the emptiness and longing be eased.

We can bring Him the brokenness of our lives and know that He will teach us how to walk in His truth until our hearts are once more made whole.

*Lord, show me when I've stepped
out of my territory into Yours.*

Psalm 87

*Indeed, of Zion it will be said, "This one and
that one were born in her, and the
Most High himself will establish her. (v. 5)*

To be established by God in a plan of recovery is real
security. Yet, most of us never realize this security
because we stubbornly cling to the old ways, the
secure and familiar methods of coping with life; and
all the while our lives become more and more
unmanageable. Real security comes about as we allow
what we have been doing to fade away and we begin
to rely completely on God. How uncomfortable that
will be at first—how frightening! Turning ourselves
over to the care of God is a real faith step, but
likewise, it is a real recovery step. It doesn't matter if
this is the first day of recovery or the twenty-fifth
year: Step Three must become a daily discipline. As
we choose to turn our lives and wills over to the care
of God, He will establish us as we continue our
journey of recovery.

*God, give me the courage to rely on You
when I want to do my own thing.*

Psalm 88

*You have taken my companions and loved ones from
me; the darkness is my closest friend. (v. 18)*

We may blame God, but, in reality it was our
addiction/codependency that took our companions
and loved ones from us. Our addiction/codependency
became a prison to our bodies, souls, and spirits; and
as we became walled in, those who mattered became
walled out. Our lives were ones of isolation and
aloneness. One by one, our significant people became
less and less important. Darkness became our closest
friend because we could hide from life.

In recovery, we become aware of our need for
companionship, knowing that getting too "lonely"
will set us up to fall again. Recovery means that the
prison doors are open, and we can begin to venture
out and rebuild old relationships in a healthy way and
begin new, non-addictive friendships. Recovery
dispels the darkness as we learn how to nurture those
in our lives.

*Lord, please begin to remove those
walls of isolation, brick by brick.*

Psalm 89

*I will sing of the Lord's great love forever; with my
mouth I will make your faithfulness known through
all generations. I will declare that your love stands
firm forever, that you established your faithfulness
in heaven itself. (vv. 1-2)*

One way to carry the message of recovery is to share
all of the struggles *and* victories. Another way is to
tell of God's faithfulness. Reaching out to fellow
strugglers by sharing our stories of recovery refreshes
our hearts. To remind ourselves that our Father was
faithful even when we couldn't believe, even when
we failed to make positive steps, not only encourages
others, but also builds our faith in God. To realize
that we all walk along similar pathways and share
common feelings is helpful. When we are able to be
honest about bad days, others realize that what they
experience is a normal part of recovery; and they are
more able to relax.

Listening to others always helps us keep our
bearings. So today, look for someone who may be
having a difficult time and reach out to that one. It
will strengthen your own personal recovery.

*Lord, give me creative ways of taking
the message of recovery to others.*

Psalm 90

*For a thousand years in your sight are like
a day that has just gone by, or like a watch
in the night. . . . Teach us to number our days
aright, that we may gain a heart of wisdom.
Relent, O Lord! How long will it be? Have
compassion on your servants. (vv. 4; 12-13)*

A child on a family outing often asks, "Are we nearly there? How much longer?" In recovery, we often forget that we are not heading toward some goal where, once we have arrived, we stop working and relax. Recovery is a daily life-style; even when we have been sober for several years, we keep working the Steps.

God is not on our timetable, and He doesn't watch the calendar to see how long it has taken us to attain a certain plateau. He has all of eternity. If we work the program faithfully today, we are recovering. So why worry about the time frame?

When we remember that today is all we have, we are able to do whatever assures us of living sober lives each day. When we live one day at a time, we learn to enjoy where we are, to enjoy this day. We stop letting our yesterdays or tomorrows steal today.

*Lord, help me concentrate on today's Steps
and not let tomorrow steal today.*

Psalm 91

He will cover you with his feathers, and
under his wings you will find refuge;
his faithfulness will be your shield and rampart. . . .
Because he loves me, says the Lord, I will rescue
him; I will protect him, for he acknowledges
my name. . . . With long life will I satisfy him
and show him my salvation. (vv. 4; 14; 16)

We must dwell, live, and abide in the shelter of God and rest in His shadow. He is our only fortress, our only refuge; and we make the choice to trust. He will save us from addiction/codependency and from the aftermath of destruction of that manner of living. We can take refuge under His wings. Remembering His faithfulness will shield us. To live in God—inside God, in Jesus, to really live there—insures us that no harm or disaster will destroy us. Most of us think that God is our guarantee against trouble, struggles, pain, or disappointment. He is not. But He does say He will be with us in trouble; He will hear us when we call on Him; and He will show us His salvation, deliverance, hope, and victory.

Father, teach me to abide in You during
stormy times as well as sunshiny days.

Psalm 92

It is good to praise the Lord and make
music to your name, O Most High,
to proclaim your love in the morning
and your faithfulness at night. (vv. 1-2)

Maybe not today, but one day when recovery is well established, we will find it good to praise the Lord. We will then tell other addiction/codependent people about the hope of recovery. We will be able to tell those who have not yet committed themselves to a program of recovery that God loves them *as they are*. We will be able to tell others that He is faithful even in the midnight of our discouragement, that He never leaves or forsakes us even when we scream at Him in our anger. It is this message that Step Twelve encourages us to share. We will live to see our enemy, addiction/codependency, defeated. Our lives will still count. We shall yet be free: recovery does happen.

O God, remind me that recovery happens
if I allow it to happen.

Psalm 93

The Lord reigns, he is robed in majesty; the Lord is robed in majesty and is armed with strength. The world is firmly established; it cannot be moved. (v. 1)

The Lord reigns! What a statement of recovery. As long as we try to reign or control, recovery will not continue. When we allow God to be in charge and reign over us, then we progressively experience recovery. Sounds so easy, but in reality it is one of the most difficult tasks in recovery. When we allow the Lord to reign, we surrender our wills, our plans, even our lives. To admit we are powerless is very hard, but to actually resign as "boss" and allow God to direct is frightening. Yet, peace comes when we give up. We may come to a place of allowing the Lord to reign today, but it is easy to reclaim our position if we are not careful.

Today, the Lord reigns in our recovery. Today, we will experience peace.

Lord, when I hate to give up, let go, or turn it over, please give me strength.

Psalm 94

O Lord, the God who avenges, O God
who avenges, shine forth . . . . The Lord knows
the thoughts of man; He knows that they
are futile . . . . Unless the Lord had given
me help, I would soon have dwelt in
the silence of death. (vv. 1; 11; 17)

We want God to take vengeance, and we would certainly enjoy being on the "God squad" when He does take vengeance on those who have hurt us. How completely normal to feel this, and yet, while we hold on to our grievances and hope that "they get their just rewards," we aren't moving forward in our recovery. Is it worth it?

Stinking thinking is completely futile, and God is always working to help us see that our sick thinking will keep pulling us back into those old ways. God wants to teach us how to change those negative, defeating thought patterns.

Addiction and codependency are progressive and terminal diseases. We may not die physically from codependency, but we are not living either. In actuality, we are dead while we still breathe—a good description of our former state of addiction/codependency. Recovery assures us that we are alive while we live.

Lord, when I want to have vengeance,
help me to release those who have hurt me.

Psalm 95

Today, if you hear his voice, do not
harden your hearts as you did at Meribah;
as you did that day at Massah in the desert. . . . For
forty years I was angry with that generation;
I said, "They are a people whose hearts go
astray, and they have not know my ways." (vv. 8; 10)

Addiction/codependency may not literally embalm us; but certainly when we are not recovering, we harden our hearts toward God, others, self, and life.

Indeed, our hearts have gone astray as we search for the next minute of relief. Our hearts stay astray as long as we refuse to surrender our lives to God.

We are able to "turn off" our ability to hear those who are concerned, and we rebelliously follow our own wills. Most of us in recovery found out that, when we follow our plans, our lives became unmanageable. When we allow God to direct us, we find peace and hope. God will help our hearts to soften and will teach our hearts to follow Him.

Lord, You are the only one who
can manage my recovery.

Psalm 96

*Sing to the Lord, a new song; sing to the Lord,
all the earth. Sing to the Lord, praise his name;
proclaim his salvation day after day. (vv. 1-2)*

Just think! A day will come in recovery when the darkness will fade into sunrise and joy will come. We will experience the emotion of joy, and laughter will come where for so long only sadness resided. Praise will come from our mouths, and we will enjoy sharing our stories of recovery with others.

Today it may be difficult to think of that ever happening, but joy is the by-product of recovery. It just happens! Recovery is a new song, and each one of us writes our own.

Begin to listen and see what the heart is singing; then sing that song over and over until it is a part of you. Today we may not feel like singing; but one day soon, our songs of recovery will become familiar.

*Father, help me look for the sunrise,
even on days when storms rage.*

Psalm 97

All who worship images are put to shame,
those who boast in idols—worship him,
all you gods! . . . Let those who love the Lord
hate evil, for he guards the lives of his faithful
ones and delivers them from the hand
of the wicked. (vv. 7; 10)

Addiction is like worshiping the chemical; codependency and emotionally dependent relationships are worshiping the person. Both are idol worship. We worship the image. We try to connect to the person and draw our lives from them. In codependent relationships, we enable . . . rescue . . . fix . . . bail out.

We put our entire lives into these people, sure that we have enough love to make them well. Nothing is too much! We don't only go the extra mile; we travel miles and miles extra. But still, we are just as sick with addiction as the alcoholic or drug addict. We are addicted to the emotional high that comes with people and relationships.

For recovery to happen, we must come to the truth that no human love is enough to bring recovery. When our "savior" complex begins to die, then recovery will begin.

O God, help me know the difference
between helping and enabling.

Psalm 98

*Sing to the Lord a new song, for he has done
marvelous things; his right hand and his holy
arm have worked salvation for him. (v. 1)*

Notice that the "joyful Psalms" are at the rear of the
book. Thank God! Most of us couldn't be joyful or
hopeful at the beginning of our journey—the pain
was too great.

But after several weeks, on some days we actually
could feel hopeful in spite of the pain.

Learning how the program works and understanding
the concepts of our Twelve Step living gives us a
promise for the future. Eventually, our emotions
begin to level out and become well enough for us to
experience some of the joy of recovery.

The best news of all is that our song in recovery will
not be a slow melancholy tune but rather happy and
jubilant. Even if we can't carry a tune, a joyful noise
will emanate from our innermost being.

O God, may my song of recovery begin soon.

Psalm 99

*The Lord reigns, let the nations tremble; he sits
enthroned between the cherubim, let the earth
shake . . . . Exalt the Lord our God and worship
at his holy mountain, for the Lord
our God is holy.(vv. 1; 9)*

"The Lord reigns" is the theme of recovery. If the
Lord is reigning in our lives, He will bring us to
recovery. On the other hand, recovery brings us to a
spiritual awakening, and we want the Lord to reign.
Either way, admitting our powerlessness over
anything helps us seek His power. To exalt means
that we place something or someone higher. To
recover means we place our Lord higher than self . . .
relationships . . . chemicals . . . food . . . sex . . .
gambling . . . nicotine.

Recovery is a style of living that constantly exalts
God over our lives—a way of life that assures victory
in recovery.

*O God, be exalted over everything
and everyone else in my life.*

Psalm 100

Shout for joy to the Lord, all the earth.
Worship the Lord with gladness, come before
him with joyful songs. Know that the Lord is God.
It is He who made us, and we are his;
we are his people, the sheep of his pasture.
Enter his gates with thanksgiving
and his courts with praise;
give thanks to him and praise his name.
For the Lord is good and
his love endures forever; his faithfulness
continues through all generations. (vv. 1-5)

As our recovery progresses, we will begin to feel better emotionally, physically, and spiritually. New days begin to be something to look forward to rather than something to endure. As health returns to us, excitement becomes a part of recovery. Gladness, worship, joy, thanksgiving, and praise become real expressions of having had a spiritual awakening, of knowing our God. At some point in our recovery, we began to see God in a different light. Rather than an angry, distant, hard-to-reach, sometimes absent God, we see Him as very concerned about us: very present with us, compassionate, and committed to our recovery. How different the relationship! In recovery, we have now truly entered into a *living* relationship, as we continuously improve our knowledge of Him through prayer and meditation. Getting well again while getting to know God—what a combination!

Father, knowing You is helping me get well.
I want to know You even more.

Psalm 101

I will be careful to lead a blameless life—when will you come to me? I will walk in my house with blameless heart. (v. 2)

Only God can make us blameless by clearing, cleansing, and forgiving us. Most of us as addicts/codependents have a tendency to want to be blameless by blaming someone else or by excusing our behavior. Blaming others has been in effect since the first couple tried to shift the blame for their choices to each other and the serpent. To blame others will not help us to recover; but taking responsibility for our actions and reactions, our behavior and our stinking thinking, will promote recovery.

Today we are responsible to walk in the Twelve Steps of recovery. We are responsible for our behavior, and our words. We are responsible. We didn't cause anyone else to drink, to do drugs, or to be codependent; but *we must face the fact* that we are responsible for ourselves.

Father, I need strength to take responsibility for myself.

Psalm 102

*Hear my prayer, O Lord; let my cry for
help come to you. . . .He will respond to the
prayer of the destitute; he will not
despise their plea. . . . In the course of
my life he broke my strength;
he cut short my days. (vv. 1; 17; 23)*

God does respond to the prayer of the destitute. As
addicts/codependents, we had reached the depths of
destitution before we were able to call on the Lord.
Because of our false pride, it was most difficult to
admit that we needed any help, and even more
humbling to ask for assistance. As long as we think
we can handle our lives, we will continue to struggle
in our own puny, weak "strength" against a giant that
is much too strong for us.

It is good news to realize that God does not despise
our plea. Because He wants us whole, He waits
patiently for our own efforts to wear thin so that we
can come to the real source of recovery. God's
"severe mercy" breaks our strength so that He can cut
short our days of addiction/codependency. Sometimes it's difficult for us to be grateful that God helps
the bottom come up to meet us rather than waiting for
us to "bottom out." In this sense, we can actually

become thankful for the pain of destitution that brought us to recovery.

O God, thank You for bringing the bottom up to meet me and for beginning the recovery in my life.

Psalm 103

Praise the Lord, O my soul; and forget not all his benefits—who forgives all your sins and who heals all your diseases, who redeems your life from the pit and crowns you with love and compassion. (vv. 2-4)

What a beautiful promise to those of us who have suffered dependency of any kind. He forgives all the messes we have made, and He heals all our diseases, even the disease of addiction/codependency. Then, to top if off, He redeems our lives from destruction.

Truly, we who struggle against addiction/codependency are oppressed. But take heart, God isn't mad at us; He never treats us as we deserve to be treated. Rather, He loves us as a good daddy or mommy loves a dependent child.

In recovery, treatment is the beginning; but recovery is a day-by-day choice that we make to work our program and depend totally on God. We take responsibility for our actions and words and live in a manner consistent with our plan of recovery.

O God, help me make the day-by-day choice to work my program while depending on You.

Psalm 104

Praise the Lord, O my soul. O Lord my God,
you are very great; you are clothed
with splendor and majesty. (v. 1)

A power greater than ourselves! This Psalm describes how great our God is. Surely a God who has the power to do all that He has done (listed in the entirety of this Psalm) can handle our recovery. The God who created this entire world, who created water and designed its boundaries, can surely handle our grief, sorrow, and tears of recovery.

Is there any doubt that He can handle our anger and confusion? God understands the emotions of our humanness, and He can teach us how to process all of these emotions in such a way as to further our recovery. God is big enough to direct our plan of recovery and faithful enough never to abandon us— no matter what we may feel.

Lord, please reassure me often that I am not
alone on this journey.

Psalm 105

*Glory in his name; let the hearts of those
who seek the Lord rejoice. (v. 3)*

Recovery happens, but it will not happen alone. We need God, and we need others. We need to find that place in Him so that we can run and hide on days when discouragement overtakes us. We need others to listen to us and give us insight and encouragement.

We need to be able to rejoice in His presence over the daily victories—as a child who has made an accomplishment or passed a test. We need other who can applaud our milestones in recovery. So our relationship with our Father God and our support groups go hand-in-hand to continue our recovery. The two together assure us that we will make it; trying to do it without one or the other makes recovery difficult and doubtful. We need God, and we need others.

Many times we ask our Father for things we are sure we need or want. We all think we know what is best for us. We tell God what we need and want. We tell Him how to run our recovery, forgetting that He knows what we need. We ask for pain or trouble to be removed, and yet it is precisely this pain or trouble that brings us to the next step of recovery. Being the humans we are, instant release from pain and pressure would make us less diligent to pursue our program of recovery.

He gives us what we need exactly—like a parent who feeds a child green beans when the child wants jelly beans. But we often fail to see how He is caring for us, even in our present circumstances.

Lord, remind me that You give me what I need to further my journey of recovery.

Psalm 106

*Who can proclaim the mighty acts of the Lord
or fully declare his praise? . . . We have sinned,
even as our fathers did; we have done wrong
and acted wickedly. . . . Yet he saved them for his
name's sake, to make his mighty power known. . . .
But they soon forgot what he had done and did not
wait for his counsel. (vv. 2; 6; 8; 13)*

Who can proclaim the mighty acts of the Lord any
better than those of us who are actively recovering?
Who can take to others the message of God's help in
recovery, His willingness to meet us at the point of
our need? We who have been there!

It's good news to realize that, even though we have
blown it, He has not ceased caring for us, loving us,
and making a way for us. God is so faithful. Thank
goodness that His love for us does not hinge on our
ability to be good or to perform.

How soon we tend to forget what He has done, and
then we find ourselves trying to run our lives, to take
charge, to manage our lives. Once more our lives
become unmanageable, and we find ourselves having
to go back to the first three Steps. Those first three
Steps were our salvation when we began recovery,

and they will once again set us on the road to recovery.

*God, I want to thank You for having
never given up on me.*

Psalm 107

Let the redeemed of the Lord say this—those
he redeemed from the hand of the foe. . . . Then
they cried to the Lord in their trouble, and
he saved them from their distress. . . . Whoever
is wise, let him heed these things and consider
the great love of the Lord. (vv. 2; 13; 43)

In our Twelfth Step, we find one of the most satisfying parts of recovery: being able to encourage someone else to begin recovery. We have been delivered from the hand of the enemy, and now God can use us to help others. Sharing our stories, being available to go to someone else with the message that God is the God of recovery, gives support to someone who is having a bad day.

In this Psalm, we see several different sets of circumstances that result in people calling out for God's help. We may have wandered in a desert of our own choosing that left us hungry and thirsty, our lives ebbing slowly away. No one could help—and then, in that desperation, we turned to the Lord. We cried out, and He heard us; but more than just hearing, He began to deliver us from our distress. We all reached the end of the rope in a different way; but when we cried out, He responded and helped.

Lord, thank You for bringing me
to the end of my rope.

Psalm 108

Give us aid against the enemy, for the help of man is worthless. With God we will gain the victory, and he will trample down our enemies. (vv. 12-13)

Addiction/codependency is a disease. True, had we not ever sampled the first drink, cigarette, drug, pie, or person, we might not have ever experienced the depth of despair that addiction/codependency brings. Yet even in our worst mess, God wants to reach out to us. Only God can deliver us.

We are not the enemy; other people or things are not the enemy. But many times we turn on ourselves, or we turn on each other, thinking we're attacking the enemy. Addiction/codependency is the enemy. Only after we properly define the real enemy, and turn our thoughts and energies to fighting not people or things but a lifestyle of death, can we begin to experience victory.

Lord, help me define the real enemy.

Psalm 109

*But you, O Sovereign Lord, deal well with me for
your name's sake; out of the goodness of your love,
deliver me. For I am poor and needy, and my heart
is wounded within me. . . . For he stands at the right
hand of the needy one, to save his life from those who
condemn him. (vv. 21-22; 31)*

Addiction/codependency indeed leaves mortal wounds
within us and in the hearts of those around us. The
wounds become even more infected when we neglect
them by living in denial or avoidance. Family
members also bear wounds because the disease and
its effect on them have stolen many precious times.
There are many broken promises. The disease is the
enemy!

Now is the time to recover these losses by making
amends where possible, making restitution where the
opportunity presents itself. Now is the time to rebuild
relationships, to express the deep feelings of love and
appreciation that we have neglected to verbalize.
Recovery sets us free to invest our lives in a better
direction.

*Lord, show me how to make restitution
and rebuild relationships.*

Psalm 110

*The Lord says to my Lord: "Sit at my right hand until
I make your enemies a footstool for your feet." (v. 1)*

Which enemies was David speaking about? He spoke
of those who chased him and sought to take his life.
Our enemies of addiction/codependency have given
hot pursuit. Had we not entered the safety of
recovery, those enemies would have stolen our lives,
joy, peace, health, and relationships.

Staying close to the Lord of recovery assures us that
we can be triumphant over these enemies. We can sit
at His right hand by meditating on His goodness,
forgiveness, mercy, patience, love, and compassion.
As we sit in His presence and become more secure
with Him, we will begin to hear the healing Word
that our Father is speaking to us. As we hear that
healing Word, our spirits are strengthened to continue
the battle. If we're failing in recovery, it's because
we have been fighting in our *own* strength.

*O God, help me realize that failure to recover
is the result of depending on myself.*

Psalm 111

*Praise the Lord. I will extol the Lord with all
my heart in the counsel of the upright and in the
assembly. Great are the works of the Lord; they
are pondered by all who delight in them. (vv. 1-2)*

Those of us who have been in the depths of
addiction/codependency and are now in the process
of recovery cannot help but praise the Lord. We
remember where we came from. With grateful hearts
we share with others our stories, our lives, and now
our hope. Remembering the past no longer sends us
tumbling into the abyss but rather reminds us that
God has faithfully brought us miles and miles in
recovery. We are a demonstration to others of God's
faithfulness to those who desire recovery. One
method of praise is to share our stories; another is to
lift our hearts and voices and tell God how much we
appreciate and thank Him for recovery.

*Lord, "Thank You" seems so small in
comparison to Your great gift of recovery.*

Psalm 112

*Surely he will never be shaken; a righteous man
will be remembered forever. He will have no fear
of bad news; his heart is steadfast, trusting in the
Lord. His heart is secure, he will have no fear; in
the end he will look in triumph on his foes. (vv. 6-8)*

Recovery brings our heavenly Father into focus. As
we begin to recover, we begin to see Him as our
friend and not an enemy. We begin to understand that
what we previously thought was freedom (doing our
own thing) actually took us into deep bondage. Only
as we acknowledged our inability to run our own
lives did we begin to come out of that terrible
captivity. Our hearts became more secure with God.
Even when bad news comes to us, we are able to
remain steadfast because we trust the Lord.

We will look back over our lives and realize that
addiction/codependency is defeated on a daily basis
as we are faithful to work our program and look to
God.

Father, You refocus life and help me see clearly.

Psalm 113

*He raises the poor from the dust and
lifts the needy from the ash heap;
he seats them with princes, with the
princes of their people. (vv. 7-8)*

If we allow Him, God can give us peace and
satisfaction no matter what we face in recovery.
Every day is not a joyful day—that is life and that is
reality. But joy does come again. Just think: Even our
bad days are not as bad as our good days were before
we began to recover. Now we are able to remember
that this day is going to pass—and with it the
emotions. Another reason to praise the Lord!

Before recovery, bad days were the only way it could
be. Our God stoops down and raises the ad-
dicted/codependent from the depths of addiction; He
takes us from the ash heap of destruction, gives us
dignity as people, and restores our self-worth and
identity. He displays us because He is delighted that
we are His children. We belong!

*O God, You have given back the dignity
and self-worth my addiction had stolen.*

Psalm 114

When Israel came out of Egypt, the house of Jacob
from a people of foreign tongue, Judah became
God's sanctuary, Israel his dominion. (vv. 1-2)

Coming out of Egypt is the same as our coming out of the bondage of addiction/codependency. God did not lead the children of Israel by the shortest, most economical route. He took them the long way home. And so it is in our recovery. He knows that we learn great lessons about ourselves, life, others, and God when we aren't instantly delivered. Our faith matures as we experience those most difficult of times and find our Father still present. Our faith muscles build as we depend on Him over and over. The lessons of powerlessness are taught again and again as we temporarily try our wings and fail. Problems in relationships and finances give us more opportunities to continue taking our personal inventories. So maybe the long road to recover is an asset after all. Thank You, God, for the slowness of recovery.

O God, strengthen me as You lead
me the "long way" home.

Psalm 115

May the Lord make you increase, both you and
your children. May you be blessed by the Lord,
the Maker of heaven and earth. (vv. 14-15)

Addiction/codependency has robbed not only from us
personally; but also from our families. Some things
that were lost in our days of addiction/codependency
were trust, confidence, and reliability. We were too
sick to hold fast to our word. We meant well, but
something always interfered.

Recovery brings us into a place with our Father
where He begins to increase and that blessing of
increase overflows to our loved ones. As recovery
continues, we are able to do what we say we will do.
Therefore, our family's ability to trust us increases.
This is a wonderful benefit of recovery. Our health
improves; and our attitude becomes more positive.
The blessings of recovery now touch not only the
addict/codependent, but also our children and other
family members.

Father, I am so glad that You can
redeem all that addiction has taken.

Psalm 116

For you, O Lord, have delivered my soul from
death, my eyes from tears, my feet from
stumbling, that I may walk before the Lord
in the land of the living. (vv. 8-9)

Addiction/codependency means three things: death to our souls, tears and stumbling. That is the progression of our disease. Outside recovery, there is no hope. Giving up all hope that we will ever be able to turn our lives around, we cried in desperation to the Lord. At the point of our greatest need, God stepped in and delivered our souls from death, our eyes from tears, and finally our feet from stumbling. The end result is that we can walk before the Lord in the land of the living.

It is easy to love the Lord because we who are in recovery are well aware that without Him, there would be no recovery. He heard us then, and He hears us now. We are encouraged to call on Him daily for as long as we live. He will always be there.

Lord, teach me that You have always
been available and You always will be.

Psalm 117

For great is his love toward us, and the faithfulness of the Lord endures forever. (v. 2)

Great is His love toward us
- when we are doing well in recovery,
- when we are struggling,
- when we feel loved,
- when we feel abandoned,
- when we believe,
- when we don't believe.

God's love doesn't depend on how well we have done spiritually. It isn't contingent on what we feel emotionally. His love doesn't rely on how many steps we have accomplished this week in recovery. His love is a gift to us, even on the days we deserve it least. God's love is unconditional: there are no strings and not one "I love you if. . . ."

Even when we don't receive His love, it doesn't stop. If we run away, His love continues to reach out and search for us. God's love is demonstrated to us over and over again, especially in His faithfulness never to abandon us and never to give up on us.

O God, thank You for loving me no matter what.

Psalm 118

I was pushed back and about to fall, but the Lord
helped me. The Lord is my strength and my song;
he has become my salvation. (vv. 13-14)

Relapse in recovery is common unless we continue to work the program and take the Steps. Many people think they are recovering because they are no longer using, but in reality, they are not living sober lives. Anytime we forget that God is the source of our sobriety, we are headed for a fall. Any day that we stop taking a personal inventory, we are backing up. If we cease improving our awareness of God, it will cause us to fall.

Recovery is growth, and unless we are growing in each of the Steps, we begin to lose ground. Even in times of danger—when we are facing or experiencing relapse—God helps us. He is our strength, and He can turn our relapses around if only we will once more come to Him and allow Him to be our salvation.

O God, help me to grow and mature in
recovery—day by day.

Psalm 119

*Your word is a lamp to my feet and
a light for my path. (v. 105)*

God's Word is essential to our continuing recovery.
As Christians in recovery, our spirits and souls need
the food that His Word gives. God's Word becomes
food when we are starving. It is the light that shines
on the pathway of recovery. God's Word is a lamp to
whatever destination we have in life.

Many times the enemy beats us with the Word, and
we think it's the way our Father feels about us. When
the Word brings fear or anxiety, it's time to remind
ourselves that God's Word

- encourages,
- strengthens,
- edifies,
- comforts,
- heals,
- delivers.

God corrects with such gentle pressure and loving
concern that we will quickly want to repent. Hope
will surround us. Don't be afraid to hear our Father's
Word today.

Lord, draw me deeper into you Word.

Psalm 120

I call on the Lord in my distress,
and he answers me. Save me,
O Lord, from lying lips
and from deceitful tongues. (vv. 1-2)

Save us, Lord, from our lying lips and deceitful
tongues. Distress is often the by-product of our own
stinking thinking and negative attitudes. Without
even realizing it, many times we talk ourselves into
distress and discouragement without ever opening
our mouths. What we meditate on—the thoughts we
entertain, the memories we rehearse—all has an
effect on what we feel. In recovery, we have a
tendency to look back at our failures, and that causes
us distress, unless we are able to also see those
failures as instruments that brought us to recovery.
Many times we view ourselves the way we were and
forget that we are still becoming. When we look
back, we must always remember to mingle in with
the memory the positive, the progress, the Steps
we've made. What was is in the past. What we are
now is important. But what we are going to be gives
hope!

O God, keep my eyes fixed on the goal of recovery.

Psalm 121

*I lift up my eyes to the hills—where does
my help come from? My help comes from the Lord,
the Maker of heaven and earth. He will not let
your foot slip—he who watches over you
will not slumber. (vv. 1-3)*

From where does our help come? Only the God of
recovery can go through each weary day, over every
mountain that seems much too steep, and into those
sleepless nights with us. Friends grow weary; loved
ones can't always be there; even members of our
support groups may not always be available. But God
will always be there! He will keep us from slipping
back into old habits. Every day of recovery God is
standing there wanting to help, yet many times we
miss that fact because of our pain or because He
doesn't do it our way or because we can't feel Him.
Nonetheless, God is a very present help in our
journey of recovery.

*O God, never let me forget that
You are always present.*

Psalm 122

I rejoiced with those who said to me,
"Let us go to the house of the Lord." (v. 1)

Improving our conscious contact with God is greatly helped by fellowship with our brothers and sisters. In the first stage of recovery, we may have avoided going to church because we were ashamed or in too much pain or it was just too much trouble. But as recovery has progressed past those days, we need that support also.

Christians sometimes have a tendency to be insensitive to others who are hurting. But never let that be said of us in recovery. We never know what may be going on in the hearts of the people sitting around us. Just a smile or an encouraging word may give others the courage they need to face their struggles. So going to church can be a twofold blessing. Our spirits can be fed as we listen, and we may be a blessing to others as well.

Lord, direct my steps to the place
of worship where I need to be.

Psalm 123

Have mercy on us, O Lord, have mercy on us,
for we have endured much contempt. We have
endured much ridicule from the proud, much
contempt from the arrogant. (vv. 3-4)

As addicts/codependents we have experienced a good
bit of contempt and ridicule from others. But the
biggest source of ridicule and contempt is not from
outside ourselves but from within. We belittle
ourselves, tear ourselves down, criticize, and hate
ourselves. Our low self-worth comes not nearly so
much from what others think and say as from what
we say and think. We speak very hurtful things in our
hearts all day long; we call ourselves names and then
wonder why we have not been successful in life. The
approval we need the most is not that of our friend,
our spouse, our parent, or child . . . *it is our own.*
Until we can accept the person that we are and love
that person and affirm that person, no one else can
make a difference. Even God's healing words will
not help. Today we need most of all to accept who
we are.

O God, give me the ability to accept myself and
appreciate what You are making me.

Psalm 124

*We have escaped like a bird out of
the fowler's snare; the snare has been broken,
and we have escaped. Our help is in the name of the
Lord, the Maker of heaven and earth. (vv. 7-8)*

Only those who have lived in the snare of addiction/codependency know how powerful that prison is. Only we who have escaped through recovery know the wonderful freedom that God has brought to us.

In the disease, the more we struggled, the more entangled we became. The more we fought, the weaker we got. But when we were truly able to realize that our only help was in a Power greater than ourselves and we turned wholeheartedly to God, then the snare was broken. In the beginning, our help was in the Lord, but also our continuing help each day is in the Lord. He is still the only one who can keep us free. The potential is there. Sometimes we are ready to fall. But if we will remind ourselves that our help is in the Lord and call to Him, He will keep us out of the snare of the fowler.

O God, protect me from the snare of addiction.

Psalm 125

Those who trust in the Lord are like Mount Zion,
which cannot be shaken but endures forever. (v. 1)

What a simple statement: Those who trust in the Lord cannot be shaken but endure forever. On the other hand, what a powerful statement: *Trust in the Lord.* What a way to declare our powerlessness and our confidence that He can restore us *and* give us courage to turn our wills and lives over to God. This *trust* gives us the nerve to allow the Lord to search our hearts. It gives us strength to confess to God our character defects and allows God to remove flaws and make restitution. It is in *trusting* that we are able to continue to understand ourselves. When we trust, our conscious contact with God improves, which helps us to pray for power to carry out His will.

Trusting in the Lord assures us that, as long as we are trusting, we cannot be shaken. No storm, no trouble, no failure can defeat us because we are trusting in the Lord.

O God, help me know that I can
trust You through whatever I face.

Psalm 126

When the Lord brought back the captives to Zion,
we were like men who dreamed. Our mouths were
filled with laughter, our tongues with songs of joy.
Then it was said among the nations," The Lord
has done great things for them."(vv. 1-3)

When we who were captive were given freedom and
were able to enjoy the fruit of recovery, it was a
dream come true. After the tears of guilt, shame,
repentance, and grief were shed, laughter began to be
part of our recovery. To laugh is to lift our spirits—to
sing lifts them even higher. To those of us in
recovery, there is much to laugh about, and to have a
sense of humor is a great asset. Laughter does good
like a medicine, especially when we learn to laugh at
ourselves. Indeed, the Lord has done great things for
us, and when we are truly aware of how much He has
done, songs of joy will come naturally. Even if you
can't carry a tune, a joyful noise will come forth.

O God, help me laugh my way through
the difficult as well as the humorous events.

Psalm 127

*Unless the Lord builds the house, its builders labor
in vain. Unless the Lord watches over the city,
the watchmen stand guard in vain. (v. 1)*

Back to square (Step) One! Humans that we are, we must continually be reminded that our lives, our plans, our biggest efforts cannot make us whole. Until we give up the struggle and make a decision to turn our lives and wills over to God, recovery will be, at best, a rocky road.

Recovery is a continual refresher course on our powerlessness and our need to turn our lives over to the care of God. How faithful He is to remind us through daily circumstances, His Word, and the Twelve Steps that we must have God as the center of our recovery.

*O God, remind me that You are
the center of my recovery.*

Psalm 128

Blessed are all who fear the Lord, who walk in
his ways you will eat the fruit of your labor;
blessings and prosperity will be yours. (vv. 1-2)

Walking in the ways of God brings blessings into our
lives. Depending on Him, turning our lives and wills
over to God brings us to a place of trust and rest.
Peace in our hearts is the by-product, the fruit of
recovery.

We cannot make anyone else in our lives recover, but
we can continue to work on our own recovery. We
can continue to walk in the pathway of recovery.
Many times the changes that occur in our lives during
recovery evoke changes in those around us. That is
also the fruit of recovery.

The best fruit that our sobriety produces is spiritual,
physical, and emotional well-being. Regardless of
what else happens, recovery leaves us much better
than when we were struggling alone. Everyone
profits when we continue the journey.

O God, thank You for the many fruits of recovery.

Psalm 129

They have greatly oppressed me from my youth,
but they have not gained the victory over
me. . . . But the Lord is righteous; he has cut me
free from the cords of the wicked. (vv. 2; 4)

For many of us, addiction did not begin the day we
took the first drink, used the first drug, or felt the first
emotional high resulting from a codependent relationship. Our addiction/codependency may have begun
years before. Part of the emotional side of addic-
tion/codependency is the fact that we never learned
how to handle pain, problems, or emotions. So we
repressed them, creating a volcano inside that was
ready to erupt.

When the emotions became so uncomfortable we
could not stand it, we began to look for something or
someone to ease the pain. It is especially difficult for
adult children of alcoholic/dysfunctional homes to
know that it is even all right *to feel.* Recovery brings
us to an awareness that God understands our emotions
and will help us deal with them appropriately.
Emotions are neither right nor wrong. What matters is
how we handle them.

Lord, I need Your assistance in
handling my emotions.

Psalm 130

*If you, O Lord, kept a record of sins, O Lord,
who could stand? But with you there is
forgiveness; therefore you are feared. . . . for
with the Lord is unfailing love and with
him is full redemption. (vv. 3-4; 7)*

Steps Four and Five are frightening when we realize
that we can no longer hide from ourselves what has
always been known by God. To see what we have
done, to realize who we have hurt, to see the debris
we have left behind is overwhelming. To have to face
this with God would be overwhelming unless we
were aware that there is forgiveness for each deed
and each failure. We are released from the guilt as we
begin to add Steps Eight and Nine to the procedure.
Although these Steps can be the most difficult of all,
there will be such freedom and healing as we humble
ourselves and make restitution. To have God forgive
us is paramount, but the completion of that act is to
acknowledge to another human our sin and failure
and then make amends where possible. God will give
us grace to do this very difficult task of recovery.

*God, give me the grace to share my
inventory with someone else.*

Psalm 131

But I have stilled and quieted my soul; like a weaned child with its mother, like a weaned child is my soul within me. (v. 2)

This was the promise God gave us personally when we began our journey into recovery. Although the journey never ends, we progress along. We find that much of the anxiety, fear, turmoil, and frustration of letting go loses its power. We also find peace and quietness filling the void.

Weaning a child is very difficult; the little one will fuss and complain and cry. But after awhile, it begins to happen. The baby finds new ways of going to sleep, and other ways to pacify himself. Nursing becomes a thing of the past, as the joy of this new developmental stage replaces the joy the child once knew with mother.

One day we will be like a child who is weaned; our souls will be quiet and still, and we will know peace.

O Lord, fill with peace the void left by addiction.

Psalm 132

O Lord, remember David and all the
hardships he endured. (v. 1)

By changing one word in this verse, we can enter into
our own personal pity party. By substituting our
names for David's, we can begin to recount all of the
hardships we have endured. We can whine and
complain and maybe even find someone else who
will listen, since a pity party without guests is quite
boring. The more we remember the hardships with a
"poor us" attitude, the worse we will feel. So why not
turn the pity party around and begin to see instead
how those hardships paved the way for recovery.
When we become grateful for things that have
happened in the past, we have taken a giant step
towards recovery.

A grateful heart is never out of style. Remember the
hardship, of course, but with a positive outlook.

O God, help me to have a positive and
hopeful outlook when I remember the
hardships that brought me to recovery.

Psalm 133

*How good and pleasant it is when
brothers live together in unity! (v. 1)*

Unity is the entire theme of recovery, the wholeness of body, spirit, and soul. When we are whole, then we experience personal unity, peace within.

Since we no longer try to control other people, circumstances, or events, we can spend that time bringing about unity in our own lives. Then we can pray that others in our lives and families will also begin and maintain a recovery in their own lives. Regardless of what others do, we can keep working our program, by taking appropriate steps of recovery and remembering that after the pain is acknowledged, rather than hidden, wholeness comes. And with wholeness comes unity.

Personal unity is often easier to attain than unity with others. But often when we have laid aside our grievances, forgiven others, and given our lives and wills over to God, we no longer have the need to get even. Therefore we may even experience unity in relationships. God is the author of unity, and He knows what needs to happen in each life for unity to happen in us.

*O God of unity, I ask You to unify
all that is fragmented in my life.*

Psalm 134

*May the Lord, the Maker of heaven and
earth, bless you from Zion. (v. 3)*

May God bless us! Whether recovery has barely
begun or we have been on the journey for a long
time, may God bless us.

May His blessings be ours on days when victory over
some habit, attitude, or problem is imminent—as well
as on those days when we are sure it will never come.

May God bless us on beautiful, clear, sunshiny days
when our hearts are light but also on days when the
clouds seem to hide the sunshine. May He bless us!

May God bless us as we live our new lives to the
fullest: as we learn to enjoy sober living.

May God bless us whether we are close to home or
must travel far away.

May God bless us with recovery, health, contentment, serenity, hope, trust, faith, love— Himself!

*God, You are the author of blessing, and I thank
You for blessings too numerous to count.*

Psalm 135

Praise the Lord. Praise the name of the Lord;
praise him, you servants of the Lord. . . . Praise
be to the Lord from Zion, to him who dwells
in Jerusalem. Praise the Lord. (vv. 1; 21)

Praise comes from the grateful heart as a natural happening. Praise comes easily when life feels comfortable; praise is not difficult when we feel like praising.

But praise can also come from our hearts when things aren't going so well for us. This is praise by an act of our wills. This praise is an act of obedience when we'd rather grumble or feel sorry for ourselves. Praise that comes from us in the most difficult, painful, and disappointing circumstances becomes a sacrifice of praise.

Even on bad days, we can praise God that it won't always be this way; things will get better. To praise our God gets us to focus on someone other than ourselves. If today is a good day, praise the Lord! If today is not a good day, praise the Lord out of our brokenness. But whatever we do, praise the Lord.

Father, please help me be willing
to make a sacrifice of praise.

Psalm 136

Give thanks to the Lord, for he is good. His love endures forever. . . . [He] freed us from our enemies, His loves endures forever. (vv. 1; 24)

Once more an entire story is contained in a few lines, but each line declares over and over, "His loves endures forever." Every story of recovery is another declaration that His love does indeed endure forever. That is why taking the message to others is so important to our recovery. Maybe that is why the encouragement to share our story is included in the Twelve Steps.

When we look back and see the hand of God each step of the way, it reinforces our trust and faith in our God. Each day we can look back and be thankful that God, with our cooperation, has kept us sober. Each story of recovery continues to make bold statements of God's love, which endures forever. From the story of Creation to the story we are now living day-by-day, His mercy does endure forever.

O God, may I never forget Your love and mercy.

Psalm 137

*By the rivers of Babylon we sat and
wept when we remembered Zion. (v. 1)*

Looking back over a lifetime of wasted years is
certainly reason to weep. Seeing the debris that we
left behind us will steal the joy and rob us of our
song. Yet, looking back is sometimes a good
measuring stick to determine our personal growth in
recovery. Looking back can also keep us up to date
on that personal inventory as we see those areas of
failure, and as we remember those we have hurt.

Have we discussed these with our sponsors and God?
Did we make amends to those involved? Have we
forgiven ourselves and others? Have we received
God's forgiveness? Looking back can be profitable if
we allow it. Looking back can give us new songs as
we rejoice because of the rescue through recovery.

Looking back can give us one more reason to praise
God.

*Lord, help me see with realistic vision the
distance You have brought me in recovery.*

Psalm 138

*I will praise you, O Lord, with all my heart; before
the "gods" I will sing your praise. . . . When
I called, you answered me; you made me
bold and stouthearted. (vv. 1; 3)*

In the early days of our recovery, we had to
concentrate on the difficult task of living through a
day without drinking, drugging, or running to our
codependent relationship. After several months, we
were able to focus on other things, other people, God,
and life. So praise has become possible for us. If the
word *praise* seems a little "churchy," try the idea of
thanking the Lord. That is what praise is, after all.
Praise God—thank God.

One of the areas of praise can always be that when
we called to God, He answered us. He began the
work within each one of us to make us bold and
stouthearted. This boldness and stouteheartedness
comes not from our own strength but because we
depend totally on God. Today we can thank Him that
He has entered into our weakness and has become
our strength.

> *Father, remind me that my weakness gives
> Your strength an opportunity to be proven.*

Psalm 139

*O Lord, you have searched me and you know
me. . . . Where can I go from your spirit? Where
can I flee from your presence? . . . See if there
is any offensive way in me, and lead me
in the way everlasting. (vv. 1; 7; 24)*

God knows us. We cannot surprise Him. Nothing we
have done or will do will catch Him off guard. He
knows our addictive/codependent nature, and He
hates what it has done to us. He is touched by our
struggle, and He has committed Himself to our
wholeness—just as much as He was committed to
delivering the children of Israel from Egypt.

Even before recovery, He was there; even when we
were so bound up in addiction/codependency, He was
there. Even when our lives were completely unmanageable and we were so "crazy" that we didn't want
Him, still He was there!

He never let go of us. Even the darkness within our
own soul does not frighten Him because He looks
through it and sees us. He is leading us in the "way
everlasting," which is more commonly referred to as
recovery.

*Lord, thank You for knowing me and
for continuing to love me anyway.*

Psalm 140

*Rescue me, O Lord, from evil men; protect me
from men of violence, who devise evil plans
in their hearts and stir up war every day. (vv. 1-2)*

When we look outside ourselves and want God to get "them," we have lost touch with the truth of recovery. It is not them we need to worry about; it is that human, carnal, old nature we still battle against. It is our hearts that will devise evil plans to sabotage our recovery. That old nature will gravitate back to the old thinking, the old attitudes, the old playmates and playgrounds. The evil that is devised is within our own hearts and will hinder us by always reminding us that we're too busy to spend time with God, that meetings are boring, that so-and-so talks too much, and we don't need the Twelve Steps.

Oh, God, rescue us from ourselves and keep us from falling. Recovery is too precious to lose now.

*O God, keep me in touch with the evil within
myself that is waiting to sabotage my recovery.*

Psalm 141

Set a guard over my mouth, O Lord;
keep watch over the door of my lips. (v. 3)

What a prayer for the recovering person. If anyone needs to have a guard over their mouths, it is those who have come this far in their journey, and forget to speak good things, positive things, and hopeful things.

What we say has a great deal to do with what we feel. The words we think and the words we verbalize contribute to our daily emotional well-being or lack of well-being.

Take a quick inventory. In the last week, what kind of thoughts and conversation have we been involved in

- with family members?
- with support group members?
- with friends?
- about recovery?
- about problems?
- about self?
- about life?

Maybe we need to change the prayer to "Set a guard over our minds and keep watch over the doors of our thoughts."

O Lord, help me clean up my
thoughts and guard my words.

Psalm 142

*When my spirit grows faint within me, it is you
who know my way. In the path where I walk
men have hidden a snare for me. Look to my
right and see; no one is concerned for me. I have
no refuge; no one cares for my life. I cry to you,
O Lord; I say, "You are my refuge, my portion
in the land of the living. (vv. 3-5)*

Does it surprise us when we're this far into recovery
to find that we still experience days when our spirits
grow faint? Are we dismayed to find that everyone
isn't excited about our recovery, meetings, Steps, and
God? Does it cause us to fall by the wayside when
something trips us and we fall? When we try to run
back to something comfortable and it no longer feels
secure, are we disappointed? We will fail; others will
fail. But the good news is that God knows where we
are walking, and He doesn't lose sight of us for even
a minute. Though no one else is concerned or offers a
refuge, *God does care,* and He is our refuge. Life is
full of disappointment and problems, and recovery
does not change that. But recovery does equip us to
deal with life in a more mature way.

*Father, give strength to my spirit to deal
with life in a more mature manner.*

Psalm 143

*I remember the days of long ago; I meditate on
all your works and consider what your hands have
done. I spread out my hands to you; my soul
thirsts for you like a parched land. (vv. 5-6)*

To remember what our lives were like before
recovery can be painful, but to add the works of God
in our lives makes it positive. Just to think about
where we have been brings us down, but to see where
we are going gives hope. So always combine the two:
what we are and what God is making us; where we
were and where God is taking us; life before recovery
and life on the journey of recovery.

As we grow in our recovery, our souls become thirsty
for more of God. We reach out to Him as a child
asking for water on a summer day. As we remind
ourselves of God's work in our lives, how can we not
want to know Him more? After all, look at the place
from which He has rescued us!

*O God, knowing You causes me
to want to know You more.*

Psalm 144

*Praise to the Lord my Rock, who trains my hands
for war, my fingers for battle. He is my loving
God and my fortress, my stronghold and my
deliverer, my shield, in whom I take refuge,
who subdues peoples under me. (vv. 1-2)*

The God of recovery, the God of new beginnings, the God of our lives—and what a God He is! When we are unstable, He becomes our rock. When we are defeated in the war, He teaches us how to do battle. When we are exposed to those who want to wound us, He surrounds us within the fortress of Himself. He is a stronghold, a deliverer, a shield in whom we can hide. Yet He is a God who helps us turn around and face our greatest enemy: ourselves.

He is a God who can be depended upon no matter what is going on in our lives. The God of recovery is our true friend.

Lord, let me turn to You as my best friend.

Psalm 145

The Lord is gracious and compassionate, slow to anger and rich in love. The Lord is good to all; he has compassion on all he has made. (vv. 8-9)

Many times our idea of God is distorted by wrong belief, and often that perception hinders our having a good relationship with Him. As we seek to improve our conscious contact, we have two possibilities. We can meditate on what we thought God was, or we can meditate on what He tells us about Himself.

In this Psalm, we see that He is good, righteous, gracious, compassionate, slow to anger, rich in love, and good to all. Stop and think: How does this God compare to the God of our perception? With which God would we find it easier to build a close relationship? Since our meditation builds our trust or destroys it, we can see how important our perception is. Lord, give us a true knowledge of You.

O God, help me meditate daily on what You tell me about Yourself.

Psalm 146

*Do not put your trust in princes, in mortal
men, who cannot save. . . . Blessed is he
whose help is the God of Jacob, whose
hope is in the Lord his God. (vv. 3; 5)*

We codependents find it most difficult to turn our
attention away from "mortal men." We addicts find
it more difficult to stop expecting others to take
responsibility for us. But true recovery will bring
each of us to these points of awareness soon enough.

No one, regardless of how much they love or care
about us, can guarantee to always be there. No one
can save us from addiction/codependency; no one can
walk the road of recovery with us. This forces us to
look to God for our help. God will not fail us. He
remains faithful, sets prisoners free, encourages us
when we are down, and will always walk with us. He
is our guarantee of recovery.

*O God, help me stay on track knowing
that a mere human will fail me.*

Psalm 147

He heals the brokenhearted and
binds up their wounds. (v. 3)

Many of us have experienced wounding that left us
with broken hearts and damaged emotions. Had our
wounds been ones that could be seen with the eye,
such as a cut or a broken bone, we would have
known what to do to facilitate healing. Broken hearts
and emotional wounds are often left for time to heal,
simply because we don't know that God wants to
heal our emotional hurt too.

Part of recovery is to face the truth of our lives,
whether it is wrongs we have committed or wrongs
done to us. It is this truth, along with the truth of
God's Word, that sets us free. Yes, this is usually
very painful, but this is a healing pain. As we see the
hurts, we can bring them to Jesus, who will gently
clean and wash those wounds so that healing can take
place. No wound is too grave nor is any scratch so
minor that He isn't concerned. Today, bring that
broken heart to Him, knowing that as that deep
emotional wounding is touched by Him, recovery and
wholeness become more and more obvious.

Lord, I bring all the brokenness in
my life to You for healing.

Psalm 148

Praise the Lord. Praise the Lord from the heavens, praise him in the heights above. (v. 1)

Praise the Lord! He has given us at least one hundred forty-eight days of sobriety. He has reached into the deepest pit and brought us into a land of hope and light. He has walked with us in the sunlight of recovery and the darkness of discouragement. He has carried us when we could not walk, and He has encouraged us when our steps faltered. Our God has given us His healing Word for our diseased bodies, souls, and spirits; and He has helped us walk out our sickness. If God has given us one hundred forty-eight days in recovery, then we can trust that He will not abandon us; He will continue to walk with us.

Praise the Lord for hope, help, healing, and hearing us when we cry out. Praise Him for love, grace, and mercy. Praise Him for the journey of recovery. Praise Him for our own personal songs of recovery. Praise Him!

Lord, I praise You for another day of sober living—Your gift to me.

Psalm 149

For the Lord takes delight in his people;
he crowns the humble with salvation. (v. 4)

The Lord delights in His people. Could that be true? God delights in each one of us whether we deserve it in our own estimation or not. God places a high value upon us. We would go to the ends of the earth to have a person's approval, to know that someone special thought well of us. We work extra hours and go miles out of our way to do something nice for someone because we want to feel good about ourselves. The God of this universe, the King of Kings, thinks we are a delight. A mother and father look at their little baby: no hair, wrinkled skin, and no control over muscles, bladder, or bowels. That child is theirs; and although he or she can give nothing, do nothing, and has accomplished not one thing, those parents love their child just because the child is. As those parents love that child, our Father loves us, delights in us, and wants to bless our lives with salvation from our addiction/codependency. He crowns us with the gift of recovery.

O God, thank You for Your opinion about me,
even when I don't measure up to it.

Psalm 150

*Let everything that has breath
praise the Lord. Praise the Lord. (v. 6)*

One hundred fifty days of recovery! Maybe a few months ago, as we began this journey, we were not sure we would get past the "getting clean" stage of recovery. We lived through that, and then came the pain of staying clean on difficult days. God was faithful to us on those difficult days. As we have faithfully worked the Twelve Steps—over and over—our spiritual, emotional, and physical well-being has strengthened. Now, months into recovery, we know that recovery is a life-style to maintain rather than a goal to be reached. We have come to know that our powerlessness is a blessing that helped us turn our lives and wills over to God. This gave us courage to take a moral inventory and share it. Next came the removal of defects of character and short-comings. Then, building on the foundation: the continuing growth of recovery began: taking on-going personal inventories, improving conscious contact with God, and sharing our stories of recovery with others. This has worked for hundreds of thousands of people, and it will work for us.

Praise God, who is the author of recovery!

Lord, I thank You for men and women
who are living testimonies,
and that I, too,
can make recovery my life-style.